Witch Crafts

Witch Crafts

101 Projects for Creative Pagans

WILLOW POLSON

CITADEL PRESS
Kensington Publishing Corp.
www.kensingtonbooks.com

CITADEL PRESS books are published by

Kensington Publishing Corp.
850 Third Avenue
New York, NY 10022

All Kensington titles, imprints, and distributed lines are available at special quantity discounts for bulk purchases for sales promotions, premiums, fund-raising, educational, or institutional use. Special book excerpts or customized printings can also be created to fit specific needs. For details, write or phone the office of the Kensington special sales manager: Kensington Publishing Corp., 850 Third Avenue, New York, NY 10022, attn: Special Sales Department, phone 1-800-221-2647.

Citadel Press and the Citadel logo are trademarks of Kensington Publishing Corp.

First printing: November 2001

10 9 8 7 6 5 4 3 2 1

Printed in the United States of America

Library of Congress Control Number: 2001092055

ISBN 0-8065-2247-X

This book is for all who love the Old Ways and who love to create beautiful things.

May you find inspiration in the East; may you find motivation in the South; may you find contemplation in the West; and may you find satisfaction in the North.

May the Great Spirit guide your hands and Ma'at guide your heart. Blessings on your path.

Contents

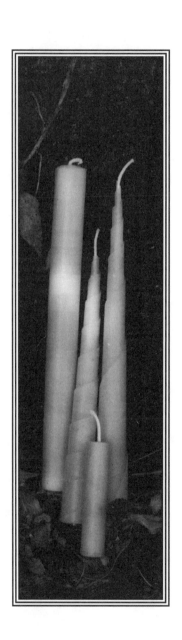

Preface

The morning is chilly. The people gather around the fire at the front of their cave for both warmth and food. They are concerned with survival, as winter is drawing in quickly. All eyes suddenly shift to the large hide flap at one edge of the cave's wall. An old man emerges, holding something within his gnarled and scarred hands. He approaches the fire with a look of serene confidence and reveals his treasure. In his dark hand glows the white carved image of a woman, rounded with plenty, her face left blank since no one can truly see the face of the Goddess. The people gaze upon this mystery he has been coaxing from the ivory all through the night and know that She will not abandon them.

And so it continues, season after season, year after year, eon after eon, to the present. We love our Lord and Lady just as much as those people on the path to becoming *Homo sapiens sapiens* did so long ago. But times have changed greatly since the cave days, and so have our materials with which to honor the divine.

CHARMS, FOLK ART, AND TECHNOLOGY

Every Pagan knows of folk charms, spells, and images of deities made from natural materials, including herbal protection packets, wish ladders made from knotted string and feathers, and woven wheat "dollies" (harvest goddesses). Most of these are quite ancient in materials and intent, as can be expected.

In successful cultures where people had more leisure time away from the business of survival, and especially where royalty existed to commission great works, the arts flourished. Some obvious examples of this are ancient Egypt, Crete, the Americas, Greece, and China. With the increasing dominance and wealth of Christendom, under the kings and queens of the Middle Ages and the Renaissance, the world gained such works as the Book of Kells, the Vestments of the Order of the Golden Fleece, and the masterpieces of Botticelli, Michelangelo, da Vinci, and others.

Many of these advances in art were due to advances in technology. For example, Native American beadwork did not exist until glass trade beads were brought to them from Europe. Constant advances in the development of permanent paints made the Sistine Chapel possible, and it is an interesting lesson for the art student to observe the broadening of the color palette from simple earth pigments to today's rainbow of bright acrylic paints, and even fluorescent colors.

The modern Pagan craftsperson has many art forms to choose from indeed! Modern Pagans are also real people, and most are looking for a fun hobby with readily available materials to fulfill their creative urges as opposed to casting bronze monuments in their backyards or grinding up rocks to make paint. It is to today's home crafter that this book is dedicated. The most involved projects in these pages require some woodworking or ceramics equipment, but most can be created with materials from any craft store in just a few hours.

FROM MUNDANE TO SACRED

What differentiates an ordinary piece of art from a sacred object? Intent, purpose, and use. Every turn of the potter's wheel, every stitch of the needle, every stroke of the brush can be filled with magical intent, creating a charged, sacred item as you work. You can enhance this in a myriad of ways, from listening to spiritual music, to repeating a chant or mantra, to taking a ritual bath before you begin each time.

The purpose of the item is also important. You can craft an attractive wooden staff to aid you when walking, or you can create a ritual staff, to be used only at certain times, adorned with antlers, fur, feathers, shells, or anything else that has deep meaning for you. Obviously these two staffs are very different in many ways, especially when you craft the ritual one with energetic intent.

The final key to the triad is the use of the item. I have seen many beautiful sacred items that end up being little more than "altar dressing," and I'm guilty of this myself. What good is a ritual or spiritual item if it's just an object in the corner? If the intent during creation is there, and the purpose for it is sacred, then the use of it in a magical way seals the spell. Make a quilt of protection and use it for protection on your bed. Create an offering bowl and leave offerings in it. Form some magically attuned candles and burn them during a ritual.

These projects are designed to be fun to make and to add to your magical "bag of tricks." In coming up with ideas, I thought about what I've needed to use myself, seen at a public ritual, or never been able to find (among other inspirations). But there's also plenty of projects that are just for fun too. Make them to be enjoyed every day as you walk the Pagan path, not just in a ritual context.

The designs are generally arranged in each chapter from easy to difficult, and at the end of each chapter will be tips, techniques, suppliers, and diagrams to help you create like a pro. Many of these projects, especially the simpler ones, are perfect for gift giving, giveaways, group projects, and even for children to try (with adult supervision).

Certainly, whole books have been devoted to the topics covered in each of these chapters, so think of the projects herein as your jumping-off point rather than the end-all and be-all. Feel free to invent variations, try different materials, adapt a design to your needs, and get creative!

Acknowledgments

Without the kind support, assistance, and inspiration of the following people, this book would not have been possible: my dear husband and soulmate, Craig, who watched our son when I needed to work, thought my ideas were very cool, and told me I was beautiful; my friends in Luna Circa and House of Life, including Denise, Jen, Mary, Shells, Tina Marie, Monet, Victoria, and Creatress; my sister, Karen; my friends at EGW Publishing, who taught me so much and so well, especially Judy; Aylene of the Running Thread (the best needlework shop anywhere!); Carol, of the South Bay Calabash Society, who graciously supplied me with free gourds; and the extremely nice people at Springfield Leather Co., Keepsake Quilting, Sacred Source, and D&J Hobby. Long live the independent craft-supply shops around the world!

Witch Crafts

CANDLES

Tired of buying those boring, ten-to-a-bag tapers with no personality? Don't want to keep shelling out the price of a good sandwich for one pillar candle? Easy! You can make your own candles in the kitchen for just pennies, and perhaps more important, craft them so they're magically attuned to your needs.

THE BASICS OF WAX

Most candles are made of paraffin, a by-product of petroleum. You're probably familiar with the little blocks of it you can get in the supermarket for canning jelly, but this is definitely the expensive way to go. You should order large blocks from a candle supplier—it's much, much less expensive. Wax from the supplier comes in 11-pound cakes, and you can order half cakes if you plan to make only a few candles. Don't be confused by all the melt point temperatures in the supplier's catalog—go by the description of what you want it to do and you'll be fine. Paraffin burns cleanly, is easy to color, and usually doesn't drip. It's also much less expensive than beeswax, unless you're lucky enough to know a beekeeper.

Beeswax has a wonderful fragrance of its own, is a natural product, burns cleanly, and can be easy to work with when you use roll-up sheets. You can buy beeswax in cake form, usually in 1-pound blocks, or in the decorative honeycomb-patterned sheets. The sheets are usually available in a variety of bright colors as well. On the downside, beeswax does drip, and, as mentioned above, can be much more expensive than paraffin. Beeswax is also more difficult to tint due to its honey color, and the sticky wax can be really hard to remove from most surfaces. But I still love beeswax due to its fragrance, natural origins, and "traditional feel."

A few more exotic waxes are available, such as carnauba (vegetable) and traditional bayberry. The more common varieties, from the bee and the refinery, are the only ones covered here, however.

SUPPLIES

To melt and work with any kind of wax, you'll need a few basic tools that will need to be dedicated to your purpose—not a magical dedication, a practical one, because you don't want to cook with waxy pots and pans.

YOU'LL NEED:

Old double boiler or medium saucepan you don't need anymore

Large coffee can (or #10 food can) with one intact end and one open end

Wax

Large knife

Several unwanted hot pads

Assorted molds of whatever shape you like

Braided and paper-core candle wicking (string only looks like it will work—don't use it)

Crayons or commercial dyes

Essential oils or commercial fragrances

Herbs

Some heavy washers

Ice pick

A package of mold sealer putty (nonhardening modeling clay will melt)

A note about wicking: There are many shapes and sizes on the market, and there are really only a few things you need to know. If you need the wick to stand up on its own before the wax is poured, use a paper-core wick or, if you prefer wire-core, be absolutely sure that the wire inside the wick does not contain lead. The only rule about flat or square braided wicking is "the thicker the candle, the thicker the wick." Use thin wicking for small candles and dipped tapers, thick wicking for large molded candles. Of course, with every rule there's an exception—for large candles that have multiple wicks, use a medium-weight wicking rather than a thick wicking.

GETTING STARTED

The following method of melting wax should be used for any kind of wax. Use your large knife to break up a large cake of wax into 2- or 3-inch chunks. On the stove, place the coffee can inside the saucepan and fill the can with the wax chunks. Fill the saucepan with water to about 2 inches from the top, and turn the burner on medium. As the water begins to boil and the wax really starts melting, turn the heat down to low and keep an eye on your wax. The water should be at just a low boil, and the wax should continue to melt. If the heat is too low, the wax will start getting a very thin skin on top—that's your cue to turn up the heat just a bit.

Here's a trio of safety rules:

1. Don't let the water boil too violently.
2. Never let the pan boil dry.
3. Never leave the hot wax alone on the stove, as it is very flammable and, if overheated, can burst into flames.

Check your wax, melting chunks as needed to fill your mold. More is better here—you can always reuse extra wax, but you can't fill a mold with nonexistent wax. Add your dye (or crayons) and scent (or essential oils), and when the wax is all melted, stir it well to blend the color and scent into the wax. When your mold is ready, turn off the stove, grab the can with two potholders, and slowly pour the hot wax into your mold. That's all there is to it! All that's left to do is let the wax cool completely and remove it from the mold.

THE PROJECTS

EMBELLISHED NOVENA

This is about as easy as it gets for the candle part, plus you have the fun of picking out images to attach to the glass for a beautiful stained-glass window effect. If using a premade candle, you will need only the first three items below.

YOU'LL NEED:
> Medium-weight wicking
> Small stone or large washer
> Heavy glass jar or premade plain novena candle
> Pencil or stick wider than the mouth of the jar

Wax, enough to fill the jar
Crayons or purchased dye (optional)
Japanese rice paper, colored tissue paper, gift wrap,
    silk flowers, etc.
White glue or decoupage medium

If you're making your own jar candle, tie the wicking to the stone or washer, drop it into the jar so it's centered, and tie the other end to the pencil so that the pencil rests across the mouth of the jar. Melt the wax, add crayons or dye, stir, and pour it into the jar carefully and slowly. (Pouring too quickly can cause the jar to crack and push the wick off-center.) Allow to cool completely and trim the wick.

Use a variety of papers, silk flowers, etc., to decorate the glass; attach them with the glue or decoupage medium however you like. My examples feature flowers clipped from gift wrap, torn bits of tissue paper, torn scrapbooking vellums, and silk leaves. Don't worry that the paper will catch fire—the glass will never get that hot. (For illustration of finished project, see color photo-insert.)

ROLLED BEESWAX TAPERS

These candles are so easy to make you won't believe it, and they may prove to be an addictive hobby for the whole family.

YOU'LL NEED:
    Knife or scissors
    Light- to medium-weight wicking
    Beeswax sheets, any color or pattern (one per candle)
    Ruler or straightedge (optional)

Cut the wick about 1 inch longer than the short side of a wax sheet and lay it along the edge. Curl the edge carefully over the wick and press into place, then begin rolling the wax sheet into a taper. If you have trouble rolling the sheets and they tend to crack or roll unevenly, the room is too cold. If the pattern crushes too easily or you leave fingerprints, the room is too warm. Test the size in a taper candleholder, cut off any excess, and press the edge firmly to stick it down.

To get a little more creative, roll two different-color sheets together, using the ruler cut a sheet at an angle to make a spiral candle, or experiment with flared edges.

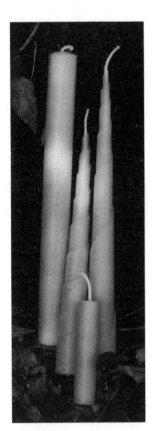

Rolled Beeswax Tapers

Witch Crafts

COLOR CARVED LOTUS PILLAR

Any design you like can be carved into these candles, but be absolutely sure the candle you're buying has a white core and has been overdipped with a darker color; if you're not sure, check the bottom or wick for signs of overdipping. You can also make your own by dipping a white candle of any shape or size in several layers of very dark colored wax.

YOU'LL NEED:

> Overdipped dark blue 4-inch pillar candle
> Paper towel or nylon stocking scraps
> Pencil
> Small U-gouge hand carving tool

Lay the candle on your paper towel. Lightly draw the pattern on the candle with the pencil to make an ultra-fine line. Follow the lines with the gouge, altering the angle of the blade as needed to create a graduated groove. Go slowly and take tiny shavings off with each pass. If you try to rush or dig too deeply you will either crack or remove the colored layer accidentally, or you could slip and ruin your design with a big scratch (or blood). By taking a little off at a time you will also be able to see when you are beginning to cut through the colored layer to the white layer below and make a nicely shaded transition. When you're finished, gently pick off any loose wax and lightly buff the candle with the towel or stocking.

Color Carved Lotus Pillar

Pattern for Color Carved Lotus Pillar

HARVEST GEL CANDLE

A really popular new way to make candles is with gel, which can be colored with special dyes and fragranced any way you like. I chose to present a harvest motif "in the round."

YOU'LL NEED:

> 23-ounce jar gel wax
> Glue gun and glue sticks
> 4-inch nonlead wire-core wick clip
> Medium-size clear glass bowl
> Assorted harvest-theme buttons (without obvious holes)

In a medium saucepan, melt the entire jar of gel wax over low heat according to the package directions. While the wax is melting, use hot glue to secure the wick clip in the center of the glass bowl. When the wax is melted, pour a 2-inch layer in the bottom of the bowl and allow to partially set. (It should still be somewhat liquid in the center.) Stand the buttons up in the gel along the outsides of the bowl; I alternated large and small buttons and kept similar designs on opposite sides so that there is no front or back to the candle. Pour in the rest of the wax, or enough to fill up to 3/8 inch from the top of the wick. Straighten the buttons as needed, wiggling them a little to help get rid of excess air bubbles. Keep an eye on them to be sure they don't fall over as the hot wax softens the first layer, but don't move them too much because the dye might not be colorfast when in contact with the gel. Allow to cool completely. (For illustration of finished project, see color-photo insert.)

BASIC MOLDED CANDLE

This is probably the most common way to make candles, and once you get the technique down, the sky's the limit. You can even use candy and cake molds!

YOU'LL NEED:

> Small milk carton or purchased candle mold
> Wick appropriate to the size of your mold
> Mold putty
> Pencil
> Wax, enough to fill the mold
> Crayons or purchased wax dye
> Essential oils or candle scent (optional)
> Sharp knife

For the milk carton, poke a small hole in the bottom for the wick, thread the wick through, seal it well with mold putty, tie the other end to a pencil, and rest the pencil on the top of the carton to hold the wick taut. A purchased mold will already have a hole in the bottom, so just insert the wick, seal it, and tie it to a pencil as above. Carefully pour in the melted wax and allow to cool about 30 minutes. Use a sharp knife to cut a hole in the bottom of the candle and reveal the liquid wax in the center, then add more wax to fill in the dent that is created as the wax cools and shrinks. Don't allow this fresh wax to exceed the height of the original candle—it doesn't look good and makes it hard to remove the finished candle from the mold. Now just wait for the candle to cool completely and slide it out of the mold (or, if using a milk carton, tear off the carton).

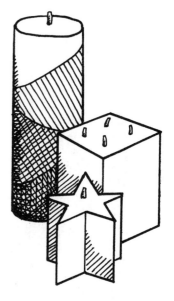

Basic Molded Candle

VARIATIONS:

To make diagonal layers, simply tilt the mold, pour in a small amount of the first color, and let it cool. Then tilt the mold the other way, pour in a second color, and so on until the mold is full (just remember to make the last pour vertical).

Concentric layers are pretty easy but can be a little tricky if you don't time it right. Here, pour the mold full of whatever color you want on the outside and let it cool until you have about half an inch of wax that's solidified around the outer edge. Carefully cut a hole in the surface skin to expose the molten wax in the middle and pour out the liquid. Allow this shell to cool completely. Then just repeat this process using different colors of wax until the middle is finally filled in.

A particularly wild effect is created with ice cubes, but it doesn't always work out right, so you might have to try it several times to get just the effect you want. Fill your mold with ice cubes, then immediately pour in the hot wax, filling the mold. When the wax has cooled, pour out the water, using an ice pick to gently punch through to trapped chambers as necessary, and use a second color to fill in the "Swiss cheese" holes left by the ice cubes. Cool completely and unmold. There might still be some holes where the second pour of wax didn't reach, or even some trapped water in the middle, so if this look really grabs you, you might want to experiment with the temperature of the molten wax, or even try buying some special low-melting-point wax to perfect this technique.

Similar to the ice cube method is the chunk method. Cut cubes or other shapes out of one color of wax and evenly fill the mold with the chunks after securing the wick. Then pour a second color of wax in and allow to cool completely.

DIPPED CANDLES

You might have done this in grade school as part of the annual "Thanksgiving Pilgrim crafts" unit, and it really is very simple. For the vats, anything tall and narrow will do, like large olive oil tins or a round metal candle mold for the wax and a "family-size" powdered drink mix container for the water. Just make sure they're the same height.

YOU'LL NEED:
    Sharp knife
    Small wicking, at least 24 inches for every 2 candles
    Large washers
    2 narrow vats of the same size, 1 for wax and 1 for cold water
    Wax, enough to fill the wax vat 2/3 full
    Crayons or purchased wax dye
    Essential oils or candle scent (optional)
    Wax paper
    Taper candleholder

Cut the wicking to 24 inches and tie washers on both ends. Fill one vat with water and the other with your prepared wax. Lay a large sheet of wax paper on a clean, flat surface nearby.

Holding the wick in the middle so that both washers hang down evenly, dip the ends into the wax a few times, then immediately into the cold water. Pull the wicks straight, then repeat several times, dabbing off any excess water as needed, until you have the beginnings of two thin candles (about 1/4 inch or so in diameter). While the wax is still warm and flexible, carefully roll the candles on the wax paper to make the shape even. Continue dipping until they're about 1/2 inch thick, then roll again on the wax paper.

At this point, cut off the washers and immediately remove them from their soft wax casings to be used again for more candles. Your tapers will be wider at the bottom than at the top, which is perfectly normal—that's why they're called tapers. Now is also the time to get out a standard candleholder so you can check the diameter when they get close to the right size. Continue to dip in the wax, then in the water, until you're very close to the right size, within two dips or so. Roll one final time on the wax paper, cut off the stalactites of wax drips on the bottoms, and give your candles their final layers before carefully hanging to cool completely.

Dipped Candle

SEASIDE SAND CANDLE

This simple yet elegant candle is the perfect offering to the spirit of the sea, whether you honor Aphrodite, Mannanon, Neptune, Oshun, or the power of Water itself.

You'll need:

> 10 pounds clean beach or play sand
>
> Seashells, sea glass, small sea deity images, etc.
>
> Paper-core or wire-core wicking
>
> Wax, enough to fill the mold (low-temperature wax is best)
>
> Crayons or candle dye in blue, aqua, green, or your choice of color (optional)
>
> Essential oils or candle scent (optional)
>
> Paper cup, butter tub, or some other small disposable scoop

Wash the sand thoroughly to remove any dust, dirt, and foreign material. Then put the wet sand in a shallow container, such as a large bowl, plastic dishtub, or plastic-lined cardboard box, packing it down firmly. Find a shape you like, such as a round-bottomed mixing bowl, and after smoothing the top of the sand, press the bowl into the sand and then remove it to form an empty space in the sand that will serve as a mold. Use your finger to make three or four holes that will form legs for the candle to stand on when you're done. Add your sea items and deity images by pressing them gently into the sand along the sides of the mold, facing into the sand. Stick a paper-core or wire-core wick in the middle (or several wicks if the shape is really large), pushing securely into the sand below.

Use a paper cup to carefully pour the wax into the mold, watching to be sure you're not distorting its shape with the stream of liquid wax. Straighten the wick(s) as necessary, then allow the wax to cool completely. Carefully dig out your new candle, brush off the extra sand, clip off the excess wicking from the bottom, and check to see if any of your sea items are loose. If so, add a bit of white glue to secure them in place. (For illustration of finished project, see color-photo insert.)

WATER CASTLES

You can make castles in sand, but did you know you can make castles in wax? These are a lot of fun to make, and each one turns out different. One of the most important pieces of equipment you'll need here is a smock, as you'll get a little wet!

YOU'LL NEED:

4" taper or pillar candle

Pie tin, butter tub, old mixing bowl, etc.

Large container such as a 5-gallon bucket or larger, filled with water

Wax, 1 to 2 pounds for each candle

Crayons or candle dyes

Water Castle (*made by Jen Snedeker*)

Make a base for this candle by holding the taper in the center of the butter tub and pouring in some hot wax to a depth of about 3/4 inch. When it cools, remove the base from the tub and move it over to the large container of water, which should be very close to your supply of hot wax. You can make the castle in just one color or try using several bright colors for the spires.

Hold the base in the water so it doesn't quite go under the surface. Start by slowly pouring hot wax on the very edge of the base to anchor the tower, then slowly lower the whole thing into the water, pouring on more wax if needed. The wax will solidify instantly and will naturally form spires as it tries to rise to the top of the water. For a more wispy effect (pictured here), try sprinkling and splashing some water on top of the wax instead of letting the spires grow naturally straight and tall.

If the spires droop when you try to take the castle out of the water, let it float upside down for a few minutes so it can cool completely. Have fun as you practice forming castle towers, desert sandstone landscapes, spiraling forests, and even Spanish galleons!

SCULPTED SABBAT PILLARS

This technique is a lot of fun but can be difficult and time-consuming. An alternative is to use premade beeswax sheets, but you don't get as much of a three-dimensional effect to the flowers. The project described here is for a Yule candle, but you can use these techniques to make any kind of flowers, leaves, and other decorations. For example, for Brigid, you might want to do white and very pale pink roses on a white pillar candle. For Litha, try some small sunflowers (stick real seeds in the middle), oak leaves, and yellow roses. Harvest time is an easy one—fat purple grapes and multicolored leaves are all that's required, and you can use a melon baller to form the grapes. Experiment and have fun.

YOU'LL NEED:

Wax, 1 pound for each color

Crayons or candle dyes in red and green

2 very flat cookie sheets with raised edges

Paring knife

Tall white pillar candle

Pencil or other semiblunt tool

Heated tool, such as a glue gun, woodburning tool, soldering gun,
    or even a heated section of coat hanger (optional)

Old crockpot, potpourri warmer, or double boiler (optional)

The idea here is that you'll be sculpting partially cooled wax into the assorted shapes of flower petals, ribbons, leaves, and fruit, then attaching the shapes to the pillar candle as decoration. These really do look spectacular when finished, and they're well worth the practice you'll probably need to do them really well.

Prepare a red and a green batch of wax. On one of the cookie sheets, pour out a very thin (1/8-inch) layer of red wax and allow it to cool so that it can be handled but is still pliable like clay. Cut the wax into several 3/4-inch strips, then gently bend the strips into festively looped ribbons, fitting them to the surface of the pillar candle. Use a little liquid wax or your heated tool to attach these to the candle.

When you're satisfied with your ribbons, pour out a thin layer of green wax on the other cookie sheet. When this has cooled enough, cut out holly leaves (see illustration) and use the pencil to scribe veins in each leaf. Place each leaf in your palm and gently shape it in a natural manner so it's not flat, then attach it with hot wax to the pillar. Also make mistletoe leaves at this time in the same way (see illustration), but don't add the scribed veins. Attach these to the candle on top of the ribbon, perhaps spreading out past the ribbon—whatever is pleasing to your eye. Using the red wax, form tiny holly berries and attach these as well.

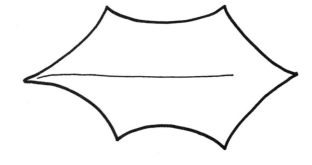

Holly and mistletoe
leaves (use for Sculpted
Sabbat Pillars)

If the wax becomes too cool, it will be hard to work with, and the edges of the shapes will be prone to cracking. To avoid this, keep the wax you're not working on in a warm oven. You'll probably need to experiment to get just the right setting, but start out at the lowest temperature you've got with the door open just to be safe. It's much easier to warm up the leaves more if the lowest setting isn't working than it is to pour a melted mess back into the pot and make a whole new sheet.

A trick you should practice for really realistic-looking flower petals is "thinning." To thin the wax, handle it as hot as possible (but not so hot that it's still liquid in the middle), and use your fingers to smooth and work the edges of your cut-out shapes, thinning them to a fine (but not fragile) edge before combining the petals to make a complete flower. This technique makes quite a difference in the realism of the flowers and leaves. Another tip is to look at photos of the flowers and plants you wish to duplicate to get the shapes really accurate and realistic. (For illustration of finished project, see color-photo insert.)

RESOURCES

Alberta Beeswax and Candle Supplies
10611-170 St.
Edmonton, Alberta, Canada T5P 4W2
(780) 413-0350
www.candlesandbeeswax.com

Alberta Beeswax is part of Tegart Apiaries Ltd., and they have a large selection of beeswax products, 100% natural waxes, and other candle-making supplies.

The Barker Company
15106 10th Avenue Southwest
Seattle, WA 98166
(800) 543-0601
www.barkerco.com

This company has everything for the candlemaker, including different kinds of wax, molds, beeswax sheets, wicking, dyes, scents, etc. In business for over forty years, it offers dependable and fast service.

Hearthsong
1950 Waldorf NW
Grand Rapids, MI 49550-7100
(800) 325-2502
www.hearthsong.com

Hearthsong carries translucent beeswax sheets for decorating candles, "Dip-a-Candle" kits, and other educational craft supplies and toys for kids.

Kewl Candle Factory
1829 S. Kings Highway
St. Louis, MO 63110
(314) 477-5258
www.gelcandlesupplies.com

This company has an amazing assortment of supplies for making gel candles, including glassware, bulk gel, blown-glass embeds, colored sand, and much more.

Lavender Lane Inc.
7337 Roseville Rd., Suite #1
Sacramento, CA 95842
(916) 334-4400 or toll free (888) 593-4400
www.lavenderlane.com

Primarily for herbalists, Lavender Lane features essential oils as well as related products such as candle-making supplies. If you only need a few items and scented oils are on your shopping list, this is the place for you.

Yaley Enterprises
7664 Avianca Dr.
Redding, CA 96002
(877) 365-5212
www.yaley.com

Since 1937, the Yaley family has supplied wax to both industry and the home crafter. Although they are primarily wholesalers to craft stores, they do sell direct to individuals and small businesses with a minimum order size of $100.00. They have everything you need to get started making your own candles.

Candle Making in a Weekend by Sue Spear, North Light Books, 1999, ISBN 1581800096

Although a little brief at eighty pages, this basic manual will get you started with lots of color photos and important "nuts and bolts" instruction on how to make candles.

The Encyclopedia of Candlemaking Techniques by Sandie Lea, Running Press, 1999, ISBN 0762406011

This book offers more advanced techniques, while still providing lots of valuable information for the beginner. Projects include "dip & carve" candles, sand casting, molding, water candles, painting, and more.

2

JEWELRY

Adorning the human body is an ancient practice. Some of the most interesting archaeological finds in history have been of jewelry, perhaps because we can imagine the person behind the object. Naturally, many of these pieces are ritual in nature, and even today we might wear anything from a simple symbolic necklace to an elaborate ceremonial headpiece.

There are many traditional materials from which to create jewelry, including metals, beads, shells, leather, gems, seeds, wire, and more. Today's crafters can also choose from polymer clay, sequins, fantasy glass and plastic beads, buttons, and other goodies from the science and minds of recent years.

When working with metals and wire, you'll need at least one pair of needle-nose pliers and a pair of diagonal wire snips, each preferably with a spring handle so it opens easily. Beaded jewelry may need a thin beading needle, or simply a length of waxed twine on which to string the beads, depending on their size. These basic tools are all you'll need to make any project in this chapter and adorn yourself for your next ritual.

THE PROJECTS

EASY HEADPIN EARRINGS

These simple earrings are quickly made with just a few supplies. Depending on what beads you use, you can make them for as little as about a dollar per pair. If your local craft store doesn't carry the styles of beads that tickle your Pagan fancy, you might need to order a few through catalogs or the Internet.

YOU'LL NEED:

Assorted beads (gemstone stars, crescents, green glass leaves, etc.)
2 head pin wires, gold-plated or silvertone
Needle-nose pliers
Diagonal snips
2 French-hook earring findings, gold-plated or surgical steel

Easy Headpin Earrings

Thread the beads of your choice on each head pin wire, matching them carefully (or, for you chaotic types, making them as different as possible while still matching colors). If the bottom bead of your choice has a hole that's too large and lets it slip off the head pin, simply add a smaller bead or a flat, disk-shaped bead at the bottom. Bend the wire over with the needle-nose pliers to make a loop, clip off the excess with the snips, and complete the loop with the pliers. Place your completed head pin wire on the French hook and close the loop, being careful to close both loops securely so they don't come apart.

A variation is to use eye pins instead of head pins, add a charm at the bottom, and thread on the beads. Twist the pin if necessary so the charm hangs correctly when the earrings are worn.

POLYMER CLAY NECKLACES

The centerpiece of this necklace is your creativity. Polymer clay is easily worked into whatever shape you like, then baked to make it hard. A friend of mine does beautiful Goddess images that look like they're made of real wood or stone by hand-blending and swirling several colors together. My example uses two cat heads, done in Egyptian style, to complement a scarab pendant I already had on hand.

YOU'LL NEED:

1 small package of polymer clay
Assorted small sculpting tools
Ice pick, paper clip, or other hole-making tool
Strong, thin cord, such as hemp or embroidery floss
Assorted beads

Work with the clay for a minute to get it warmed up and more flexible. Sculpt it into any shape you like, such as a softly curved Goddess shape, leaves, fruit, moon, animal, skull, scarab, or perhaps even a phallus. Make a hole near the top for the cord, drilling it sideways or vertically through the sculpture, depending on how the bead will be used. Bake as directed. Now, simply thread the finished bead onto your cord, finish on either side with matching beads, and tie a secure square knot in the ends of the cord, making a loop big enough to go over your head. (For illustration of finished project, see color-photo insert.)

FIGARO CHAIN CHARM NECKLACE

If you're like me, you've got lots of Pagan necklaces around and have trouble choosing which one to wear. Why not put all the charms on one silver chain like a giant charm bracelet?

YOU'LL NEED:

> Sterling silver figaro chain in your choice
>   of length
> Assorted charms
> Needle-nose pliers
> Silver or nickel jump rings

Begin by laying out where you want your charms to be positioned in the finished necklace—your favorite or the largest should go in the center—then add charms that are progressively smaller up the sides for an organized look. Don't use any that are too heavy (like that giant gemstone or pentacle hubcap) or they will weigh down the chain unevenly or even break it. Use the pliers to open a jump ring, attach it to the center charm, feed the ring through one of the open links in the figaro chain, and close the ring. You might need to use two jump rings to make the charm hang correctly, and some charms might already have a ring that you can use. Continue adding charms on each side until you have them evenly distributed.

Figaro Chain Charm Necklace

GOD AND GODDESS WIRE CIRCLETS

These two circlets are perfect for ritual uses. They can be made to fit a particular wearer so there's no chance of slippage at an awkward moment.

YOU'LL NEED:

    16-gauge copper wire (for the God)
    18-gauge silver wire (for the Goddess)
    Wire cutters
    Needle-nose pliers
    Flat-nose pliers
    Small hammer
    Small jeweler's anvil

Cut three lengths of wire per circlet, long enough to go around the head plus 2 to 3 inches extra on each end to create the hook-and-eye clasp. Make the eye by creating a small loop and wrapping the ends of the wire back around two or three times. Just hold the wires in the flat-nose pliers and twist your wrist to wrap one set of ends together as a single unit. Flatten the eye with your small hammer on the anvil.

Hook the eye on something solid, like the thread spindle of a sewing machine, and braid the three wires together, just as you would someone's hair. When you come to the last 2 inches, stop braiding. Bend the wires as a group back onto themselves so that the ends just touch the last of the braiding. Use pliers to flatten and narrow the loop. Take the free end and twist it around the body of the circlet. Fold the loop back to just below the braiding to create a hook. Flatten the entire circlet at this point if desired.

For the God's antlers, cut three lengths of wire between 4 and 6 inches long. Bend each wire in the center to make a shallow *V*, then curl and flatten each end (or the entire wire, if desired). Cut a 2- to 3-inch length to bind the antler parts together and attach them to the circlet. Hammer flat to help everything hold together.

For the Goddess's triskelle, cut one length of wire about 9 inches long. Curl one end by holding the wire in the pliers and twisting your wrist. Continue to make a flat spiral until it reaches about 3/4 inch in diameter. About 1 or 2 inches past the end of the first spiral, make a little loop and begin making the second spiral from the center outward. When that spiral has reached about 3/4 inch across, continue as though making another turn on the second spiral but turn your wrist in the opposite direction. You will have made the outer edge of the third spiral. Continue turning the wire in toward the center and then cut off any extra wire when finished. Cut a 2- to 3-inch length of wire to secure the triskelle to the circlet. Hammer flat to help everything hold together. (For illustration of finished project, see color-photo insert.)

BEADED COWRIE SHELL CHOKER

To many paths, cowrie shells represent the vulva of the Goddess and can also be used to promote fertility. The shells make a delightful sound when the wearer moves, almost like tiny wind chimes. The neckband can be altered in any way you like—you can attach the fringe to a length of loom-woven beadwork or to a wider piece of needle weaving. The colors given here are for the exact necklace shown, but you can use whatever colors you like.

YOU'LL NEED:

Thread and needle threader
Beading needles
Size 11 seed beads in iridescent red, clear yellow, and pearl ivory
1-inch glass tube beads in clear red
Predrilled cowrie shells
Clasp set and two jump rings
Needle-nose pliers

Start with the needle-woven band, which uses a simple double-strand weave. String one yellow seed bead, then three red seed beads, then one yellow, then three reds. Pass the needle through the first yellow bead and tie off the thread securely with a square knot. Continue alternating three reds and one yellow until the band is as long as you want plus about 1/2 inch. Make another loop and work your way back through the band, stringing three reds and passing through the yellow bead each time (see illustration). When you have reached the beginning again, pass through the first loop and back out through the red beads—do not pass through the yellow bead. The fringe will be strung from red beads to red beads and skip the yellows.

Cowrie Choker Neckband

Now begin stringing the shell fringe. String four yellows, one red, ten ivories, a red tube, ten ivories, one red, and four yellows. At the end, string one cowrie shell, then return back through the glass beads to end up where you started. Tighten up the strand so that no bare thread is showing, but don't overtighten it or it will be stiff or even break the thread. Go through the next red beads of the woven band, and repeat the fringe, but at the end make a loop of six yellows instead of the cowrie shell. Continue alternating fringe strands with cowries and bead loops until you reach the other end of the woven band. Pass through the loop as you did at the other end and tie off the thread. Attach the clasp and jump rings to finish the necklace. (For illustration of finished project, see color-photo insert.)

MULTISTRAND DEVOTIONAL NECKLACE

Sometimes one really special and beautiful necklace is just what the occasion needs. Pay homage to your favorite deity with this lavish collection of gemstones, beads, and charms. For example, a Laxshmi necklace would feature gold and pearls, Aphrodite would like shells and blue glass beads, and Min should be accompanied by phalluses and green plants.

YOU'LL NEED:
> 30-foot spool of .024 thickness jewelry wire
> Wire cutters
> 8 crimp beads
> 2 four-strand metal end findings
> Needle-nose pliers
> Assorted beads, gemstones, etc. related to your deity
> Charm(s) or bead(s) representing your deity
> 2 jump rings or split rings
> Lobster claw clasp set

Cut a piece of beading wire about 3 inches longer than you want the smallest strand's length to be. Thread a crimp bead onto one end a short way, then thread the end onto the first hole of a four-hole finding. Thread the wire back through the crimp bead, tighten the loop up to the ring, and smash the crimp bead flat as hard as you can with the needle-nose pliers. Turn the crimp bead over and flatten again. String on whatever beads you like for this row, but don't use any dangly ones yet. You can make it symmetrical or mix all your beads together and put them on randomly for a different look. When you're done, thread the wire through the first hole of the other finding, thread the end back through the crimp bead, tighten

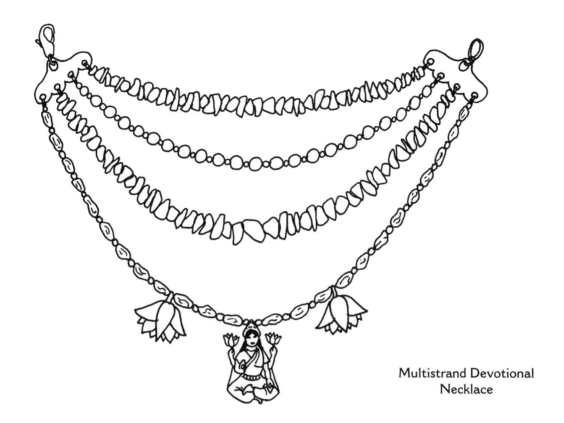

Multistrand Devotional
Necklace

the loop and the necklace, then crimp the bead as on the other end. Be careful when tightening the first row—too tight and it will be stiff or could break, too loose and you'll have unattractive bare wire at the ends.

Repeat the procedure for the second and third rows, making them progressively longer than the first. Check how the necklace will fit by placing the two findings together on the table to form a circle, or hold it up to yourself in a mirror. For the last row, repeat the procedure one more time, but now add the dangly charms and the largest beads, especially your deity images. Crimp off the row. Attach jump rings to large hole on metal end findings. Attach the clasps to the jump rings to finish the necklace.

EGYPTIAN COLLAR

Images of the *weskhet*, or broad collar, are seen on many sculptures and paintings of ancient Egypt. Denise Rogers, one of my Egyptian ritual family, spent many hours working out how to reconstruct one of these spectacular collars for our group, although the terminals are a series of modern clasps rather than drilled stone or gold. She generously showed me her technique, which, upon close examination, is almost exactly how the *weskhet* was constructed about four thousand years ago. Thank you, Denise, for letting me share this project here.

> Wire cutters
>
> 30-foot spool of .024 thickness jewelry wire
>
> 8 to12 gold crimp beads
>
> 8 to 10 small gold split rings
>
> Needle-nose and round-nose pliers
>
> 4 to 5 heavy gold clasps
>
> 200 to 300 gold-plated 2-inch eye pins (approx.)
>
> 100 gold-plated 2-inch head pins (approx.)
>
> 500 (approx.) glass size-6 seed beads, assorted colors (especially bright gold)
>
> 200 tube-shaped beads, 10mm or longer, assorted colors
>
> 50 flower-shaped glass beads or Egyptian-themed charms
>
> 12- to 18-inch-long large gold jewelry chain

The amounts of beads and pins listed are for making the exact collar pictured in the color-photo insert, sized for a smallish woman (15-1/2-inch opening diameter, worn low on the neck and shoulders). For other sizes and designs, you will need to experiment. Be sure to buy more than you think you need so you don't get stuck; I ran out of the cobalt satinas on the first vertical row and finally had to order more on the Internet after trying for months to find them locally.

Make all the beaded eye pins you will need for the first row. If you're making a design that's different from the one pictured here, make two or three of each color combination and play around with layering the rows until you're happy with the overall look. As you continue, prepare all the beaded eye pins you will need for your next row. To make the eye pins, use a production-line method to thread the desired beads on the pins, then use round-nose pliers to bend over the ends, leaving enough to make a second eye. Clip off the excess wire, then finish the eye with the round-nose pliers. After all the pins are done, use two pliers to straighten the eyes of each pin so that they are both facing the same direction (parallel).

Cut a length of beading wire about 6 inches longer than you will need for the first row. Thread a crimp bead onto one end a short way, then thread on a split ring. Thread the wire back through the crimp bead, tighten the loop up to the ring, and smash the crimp bead flat as hard as you can with the needle-nose pliers. Turn the crimp bead over and flatten again. (You can also thread a clasp onto one side directly instead of using two split rings.) Begin stringing the first row by placing one size-6 seed bead on, then alternating two seed beads and one eye pin until the eye pins are used up. End with one more seed bead, thread on a crimp bead and a split ring, thread the end back through the crimp bead, tighten the loop and the necklace, then crimp the bead as on the other end. Be careful when tightening the first row—too tight and it could break, too loose and you'll have unattractive bare wire at the ends.

Cut a 24-inch length of beading wire and thread it through the center eye pin of the first row. Now begin stringing eye pin bead sets and gold size-6 beads, threading them through the previous row's eye pins when necessary. Try to develop a regular pattern for this, such as "gold bead, row 2 eye pin, gold, gold, row 1 eye pin, gold, row 2 eye pin" and so on. You'll need to vary from this occasionally to keep the rows straight and even. String a few inches to one side, then string to the other side, then back to the first side (rather than stringing the whole left side at once, for example).

Continually straighten the collar so that it lies perfectly flat on the table, and keep a sharp eye out for any distortion in how the eye pins are lying. Use the natural variation in the sizes of the gold beads to your advantage, slightly adjusting the spacing of the eye pins. You will periodically have to unstring portions of the collar if the eye pins are beginning to lean awkwardly—they should radiate out from the center perfectly. Continue stringing until you reach the ends of both sides, then add clasps and crimp beads as before.

The last row consists of head pin dangles rather than eye pins and is strung just like all the other rows. An alternative method for the last row is to use eye pins and add a row of gold beads between the bottom eyes for a straight bottom instead of a dangly one.

When the beads are all strung, add the clasps, if you haven't crimped them in place already, by attaching them to the split rings. Add graduated lengths of chain to the other split rings—these will ensure a perfect fit when adjusted correctly. (For illustration of finished project, see color-photo insert.)

Garden of Beadin'
P.O. Box 1535
Redway, CA 95560
(800) 232-3588
www.gardenofbeadin.com

This store has a really good selection of beads, especially solid basics like seed beads, chicks/satinas, bugles, crystal, and so on. One great feature this nice little business has above other places is its sample cards, featuring real strands of beads stitched onto cards so you can see exactly what you're buying.

General Bead
637 Minna Street
San Francisco, CA 94103
(415) ALL-BEAD
www.genbead.com

General Bead carries an astonishing array of beads from all over the world with excellent prices. It features a very helpful staff and fast mail-order service, too.

Mana Beads and Jewelry
75-5799 Alii Dr., #B-1
Kailua-Kona, HI 96740
(808) 331-2161 or toll free (888) 724-2097
www.manabeads.com

This store has unusual semiprecious stone and precious metal beads, with an especially good selection of Hawaiian and Asian-style beads. They also carry findings, wire, tools, books, and lots of other supplies.

Preston J. Reuther
PMB #143
106 Gause Blvd. W., Suite 4
Slidell, LA 70460-2600
(985) 649-6505
www.wire-sculpture.com

Reuther offers a good selection of metal wires (silver, copper, gold-filled, etc.) and other supplies for making jewelry.

Shipwreck Beads
2500 Mottman Rd. SW
Olympia, WA 98512
(800) 950-4232
www.shipwreck.com

Shipwreck says they have "the world's largest selection of beads," and their catalog seems to support this claim. They also offer tools, books, findings, wire, and other supplies.

Making Wire Jewelry by Helen Clegg and Mary Larom, Lark
   Books, 1997, ISBN 157990002X

This book, complete with many photos and illustrations, is a very detailed guide for making jewelry out of silver, brass, and copper wires.

Creative Bead Jewelry by Carol Taylor, Lark Books, 1995, ISBN
   0806913061

This is truly one of the best resources for the bead jewelry maker, whether you enjoy seed beads, big beads on wire, or making your own polymer beads. The projects are varied, the text is an interesting read, and the photos will inspire you.

3

SEWING

An important aspect of ritual, and one of the hardest to find, is ritual clothing. There are a few folks out there making it, but because it's hand-made, it tends to be expensive. If you don't want to improvise with some off-the-rack street duds, you can make your own, as well as pouches, banners, and other stitched goodies for yourself or your group.

THE BASICS OF SEWING

This is one high-school class I did poorly in, but when I needed a dress for doing living history and I couldn't get it any other way, I had to knuckle down and make it myself. I did just fine when I wasn't under the pressure of getting graded and had no time restraints. If you have a modicum of patience and a sewing machine, you can make any garment you like. Of course, it's best to start simple and add techniques as you go; most ritual wear is simple enough for a beginner to make, so that's a good place to start.

If you've never sewn anything in your life, you might want to get a book on sewing for beginners. A few basic terms you'll need to know include *selvage, bias, inset curve,* and *gathering stitches*. The selvage is the machine-woven edges of the cloth. The bias is the diagonal (45-degree angle) of the cloth, and it is very stretchy. An inset curve sometimes has to be fitted using the stretchy bias of the cloth and is usually seen where a sleeve and shoulder meet or at the collar. Gathering stitches are usually machine basted, then the threads are pulled to gather the fabric, which then is stitched in place; they are usually seen on full skirts and full-sleeve shoulders.

Other things you'll need to know are what the right side of the fabric is, how to pivot the fabric on a sewing machine, what *interfacing* is, and how to clip a curve or trim a seam allowance. "Right sides together" means that if there's an obvious right and wrong side to the fabric, like a printed cotton, these right sides should face each other. To pivot the fabric, stop with the needle fully down inside the fabric, lift the presser foot, turn the fabric in the direction you need to go, lower the presser foot, and continue sewing for a nice sharp corner. Interfacing is a thin starched fabric (woven or feltlike), used to help stiffen cuffs and collars, that is available at any fabric store in a variety of colors. Clipping curves is easy: Simply make perpendicular snips in the seam allowance, allowing the curve to be turned and pressed properly. Corners must be clipped at a 45-degree angle to eliminate extra fabric that will bunch up when the piece is turned.

The kind of fabric you need will depend on your pattern or project. You might want heavy wool for a winter cloak, pure Irish linen for a Brigid ritual, or a colorful cotton harvest print for Mabon. If you don't mind synthetics, stores that carry Indian and Middle Eastern fabrics have lots of wonderful, esoteric, colorful, shimmery fabrics that drape wonderfully. Sometimes you can happen upon real metal-thread fabrics there, like real silver and real gold, and they always have lots of sheer materials for veils and special effects.

THE PROJECTS

BASIC DRAWSTRING POUCHES

Everybody needs pouches—these can be made with fabric scraps and decorated in any way you like. Have fun with embroidery, paints, glitter . . . whatever! Kids can make these, too, for a rainy day or group project.

YOU'LL NEED:

    Fabric scraps, at least 3 inches square
    Scissors
    Eyelets and eyelet pliers
    1/2 yard per pouch of thin cord, ribbon, or string
    Decorating materials

Lay two scraps on top of each other, fabric grains running in the same direction, and cut them into a neat rectangle, allowing about 1 inch extra at the top. Flip the pieces so they're right sides together and stitch (1/2-inch

Witch Crafts

seam allowance) around three sides (two long and one short), pivoting at the corners. Press side seams open. Fold top edge 1 inch toward the wrong side and press, then fold under 1/4 inch and topstitch close to the edge. Turn right side out and press.

With the point of your scissors, make eight small, evenly spaced holes in the 3/4-inch space between the top of the bag and the topstitching. Following the instructions provided with your eyelet pliers, place an eyelet in each of the eight holes. Now weave ribbons, lacing, cord, or string in and out of the eyelets, tying the ends in a secure square knot to finish. Decorate the outside of the pouch as you wish. (For illustration of finished project, see color-photo insert.)

PAINTED COVEN BANNER

Whether you're attending a large festival and need to identify your camp or simply want to have a banner up during your group's meetings, this project is easy and fun to make.

YOU'LL NEED:
>   3/4 yard solid-color fabric
>   Scissors
>   1 yard contrasting felt or fabric paints, trims, etc.,
>   for decoration
>   1 yard fringe or 3 small tassels
>   3/8-inch wooden dowel cut to 26 inches long
>   1 yard ribbon or cord for hanging

Cut the fabric into a 24-by-30-inch panel and fold in half lengthwise. On the long side opposite the fold, measure up 4" from the bottom and cut a gentle convex curve toward the bottom of the fold so that the bottom of your banner will be curved. Unfold, turn all edges 1/4 inch, then 1/4 inch again (so the raw edges are underneath), and stitch. Fold the top edge over 1-1/2 inches and topstitch close to the hemmed edge.

Painted Coven Banner

Decorate your banner with your coven emblem and designs—Luna Circa has both the dancing woman in the stars design and the yellow rose emblem, which both needed to be on our banner. I used ordinary acrylic craft paints.

When the banner is completed and any paint or glue is dry, stitch the fringe or tassels at the bottom to help weight the fabric down a little so it hangs nicely. Slide the dowel into the pocket at the top of the banner and securely tie some ribbon or cord to both ends of the dowel. The ribbon or cord will keep the banner from sliding off the dowel and let you hang it wherever you like.

SIMPLE GATHERED SKIRT

Skirts like this are ridiculously easy to produce, and can be made in the fabric of your choice to reflect the occasion. Try layering skirts of different lengths and colors, or decorating them with favorite images using permanent fabric paints (available at most fabric stores). This pattern works for fabrics with or without one-way designs or nap (like velvet), and it's a good first clothing project for the beginning stitcher.

YOU'LL NEED:

    2 yards 44-inch-wide fabric (for average-sized women; the skirt will fall just below the calf)
    Matching sewing thread
    Scissors
    Tape measure
    Straight pins
    Large safety pin
    1 yard nonroll elastic

Wash, dry, and iron the fabric. Fold the fabric right sides together lengthwise with selvages matching and trim one edge (the top edge, if using one-way fabric) so that it is square and follows the woven threads. Measure from your waist to the desired length and add 1-1/2 inches for the hem and the waistband seam—this is your total length measurement.

Cut a strip 3-1/2 inches wide from the square end of the fabric for the waistband. Measure and mark your total length measurement, then cut the first skirt panel across the width of the fabric. Lay this piece on top

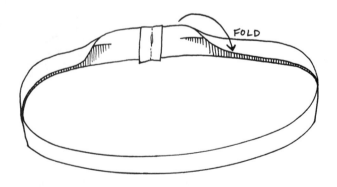

Diagram of skirt waistband

Witch Crafts

of the remaining fabric and use the bottom edge as a guide to cut the other skirt panel.

Right sides facing, stitch the ends of the waistband together, stitching a little past halfway and stopping (stitch the bottom half if using one-way fabric). Press open seam, also pressing open the unstitched portion. Fold in half lengthwise, right sides out, and press. This gives one open inner seam for the elastic to be placed inside and one outer closed seam (see illustration).

Open out the two skirt panels and match them right sides together. If you wish to have one or both sides slit, measure up from the bottom edge and mark where the stitching should end (remember to add 1 inch for the hem). (The pictured sample skirt has a 6-inch slit.) Stitch the side seams, stopping on the slit mark and backstitching at that point (or continue to the bottom if no slit). Press open seams.

Run a basting stitch around the top of the skirt body no more than 1/2 inch in from the top edge. Right sides together, match the waistband and skirt body. The opening in the waistband should face out—it will be turned inside later. Pull on the basting stitches to gather the skirt fabric so that it fits inside the waistband. Pin gathers securely and evenly, and stitch skirt to waistband with a 1/2-inch seam allowance. Press seam toward skirt body.

Attach a large safety pin to one end of the elastic and thread it through the waistband. When the elastic has made it through the waistband, remove the safety pin. Overlap elastic edges 1 inch and stitch securely in an *X* or square pattern. Fit inside waistband and stitch opening closed.

Fold the hem up 1/2 inch and 1/2 inch again to contain the raw edge. Stitch. If slits were made, pivot stitching at the corner of the hem (lift the presser foot and turn the fabric, then replace presser foot). Stitch up to where the side seam stops at the top of the slit and pivot again. Stitch across the top of the slit three times to reinforce this point and then pivot, continuing down the other side to the corner. Pivot one last time and continue stitching the bottom of the hem.

VARIATIONS:

For waist sizes larger than about 40 inches, you will need 3 yards of fabric and elastic to fit your waist measurement. Cut two waistband strips and stitch together, cut one extra skirt panel and omit slits, stitch together.

For a neater waistband, cut the waistband 1 inch wider and press the long edges under 1/2 inch. Stitch skirt body to stitched side of waistband, fold waistband in half to inside, and edge stitch to contain raw edge of skirt body. Insert elastic on inside of waistband. (For illustration of finished project, see color-photo insert.)

REVERSIBLE SABBAT CAPE

This project works best with 60-inch-wide fabric, but it can be done with 44-inch fabrics. It's a great prop for larger and public rituals. (The cape pictured here was for a public Mabon ritual and we made a great show of flipping the cloak around at the right moment to demonstrate that the wheel had turned a little more.) You can make yours one-sided with a lining or pick two different sabbats to place back-to-back. These directions are for the Mabon cloak specifically.

YOU'LL NEED:

    3 yards 44-inch-wide harvest-themed fabric

    3 yards 44-inch-wide black fabric

    Scissors

    Matching threads

    Measuring tape or string and chalk

    10 yards beaded trim in pearl, iridescent black, clear, or your choice of color

    Washable tacky fabric glue

    1 or 2 black frog closures or pewter cloak clasps

    2 black tassels

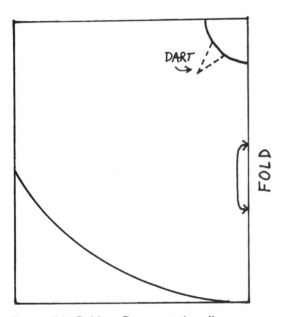

Reversible Sabbat Cape: cutting diagram

Cut the fabrics into 1-1/2-yard panels, stitching matching fabrics together at the selvages to make a 54-by-88-inch piece. Press seams open. Lay one of the pieces wrong side up and the other on top of it right side up, matching seams at center. Fold in half so that the seams are on the fold line, carefully smoothing out any wrinkles and matching selvages.

Starting at the top folded edge, use a tape measure or string with some chalk to mark an arc (see illustration) from the bottom center fold edge up to the selvage edges (60-inch-wide fabric will make a complete pie slice). From the same point, measure 5 or 6 inches down and make another arc for the neckline. Also mark two 5-inch-long darts on the wrong sides of both pieces of fabric for the shoulders. Cut on the two arc lines. Stitch the darts on the wrong sides and press. Fold over all edges once 1/4 inch and stitch. Wrong sides together, topstitch the two halves of the cloak together around all edges.

Lay out the cloak black side up. Form a spiderweb pattern with the beads, making sure to hide the center seam underneath one of the strands. Glue the web in place with the fabric glue and allow to dry completely. Try

Reversible Sabbat Cape

on the cloak and mark the clasp positions. Glue on fabric frogs or stitch pewter clasps on the black side. Glue or sew in place the tassels at the two points where the bottom arc ends, if using 44-inch-wide fabric. (Tassels are not used on the 60-inch version.)

RITUAL ROBE WITH CUFFS AND POCKETS

Most rituals necessitate the use of candles or other open fire, so this unisex robe is a safe solution because the sleeves are held to your wrist rather than hanging down where they might catch on a flame. And how many things can you think of to put in the pockets, especially at an outdoor public ritual?

Ritual Robe with Cuffs and Pockets

Pattern for "Bible play" costumes (McCall's 5568; Simplicity 8108 or 8275)

Pattern for dress with cuffs and pockets (McCall's 4555; Vogue 2326 or 1147)

5-1/2 yards 44-inch-wide fabric (approx., consult "Bible-play" pattern and add 1/2 yard)

Matching thread

Scissors

Tailor's chalk or pencil

Buttons or hooks and eyes

Trims, fabric paints, beads, other decorations (optional)

Cut out and iron flat all the pattern pieces you will need—use the simple one-piece robe view from the costume pattern and the cuff and pocket pieces from the dress pattern. Fold the fabric and cut out the pattern pieces according to the costume pattern directions, then use the remaining fabric to cut out the cuff and pocket pieces.

At your natural hipline on the costume pattern (measure down from your waistline to the point of your hip), make marks on the front and back pieces, which will be the top point of the pocket openings. Follow the directions for sewing the robe as given in the costume pattern until you get to the side seams, then pin the pockets in place according to the dress pattern, matching the pocket tops to the marks you made. Stitch the top part of the side seams as directed in the costume pattern, then switch to the dress pattern for stitching the pockets in place. Finish stitching the robe as directed by the costume pattern until you reach the ends of the sleeves.

Make the cuffs as directed in the dress pattern. Baste around the edges of the sleeves and gather up the fabric to fit the cuffs; then stitch the cuffs in place following the dress pattern. Add buttons and buttonholes or use hooks and eyes to close the sleeves.

TOPSY-TURVY DOLLS

Here are three variations of a basic topsy-turvy doll: Oak King/Holly King, Light Persephone/Hades, and Dark Persephone/Demeter. The Oak/Holly King demonstrates the duality of this aspect of the God as literal flip sides of each other. The Persephone/Hades/Demeter dolls are arranged so a child can retell this classic tale: Either Light Persephone or Hades can interact with Demeter, and Dark Persephone can be the bride of Hades (willing or not, depending on your version of the tale)—or see herself reflected as the carefree maiden of spring.

YOU'LL NEED:

- 1/2 yard unbleached muslin or tan broadcloth in your choice of skin color
- 1 yard each dress/robe fabric of your choice (harvest themes for Demeter, florals for Light Persephone, reds and dark florals for Dark Persephone, darks and blacks for Hades, harvest and winter themes for the Holly King, spring greenery and acorns for the Oak King)
- Tapestry and sewing needles
- Doll hair or yarn (I used Lion Brand Homespun yarn in "Rococo" [Persephone] and "Ranch" [Demeter and Oak King]; other good choices are "Shaker" [Holly King] and Lion Brand Wool-Ease in Black Frost [Hades])
- 1/4-inch-wide ribbon
- Synthetic or cotton doll stuffing
- Button, quilting, and sewing threads
- Craft paint in light brown, black, green, rose, and white
- #5/0 and #1 paintbrushes

Wash, dry, and iron all fabrics. Transfer the doll body pattern and the arm pattern (see illustrations) onto the wrong sides of the fabric, using a pencil or wash-out fabric pen and making sure to carefully copy the stitching line of the hands as shown in the pattern. Stitch, following the outside lines exactly; lift the presser foot and pivot the fabric with the needle down when necessary to turn a sharp corner, especially around the fingers. Do not stitch between the fingers yet. Clip curves and trim close to stitching near fingers. Turn parts right side out, using a blunt tool to work out all details carefully (the thumbs might not turn completely, but that's okay—get them "close enough" to avoid overstressing the stitches).

Using a tapestry needle threaded with yarn, stitch the hairline of the doll on the face side (whichever half you choose; front and back are identical). Knot the yarn at one end and make individual stitches 1/4 inch apart, clipping each strand to make the hair about 5 or 6 inches long. Knot the end again and repeat until the front hairline is finished; then start on

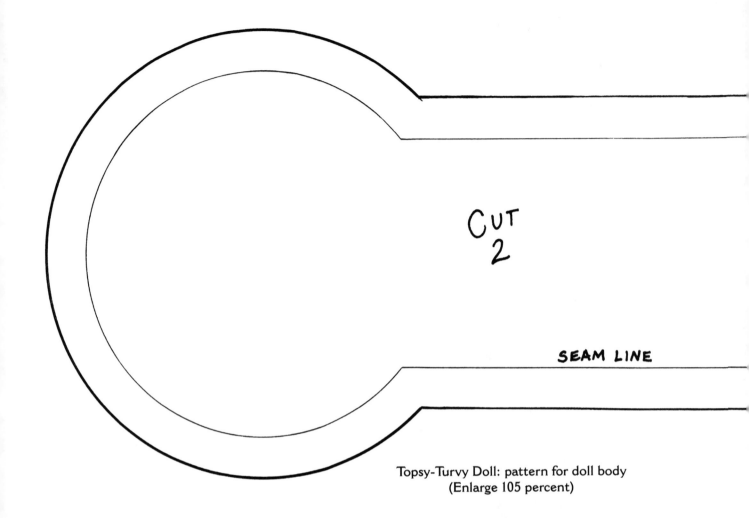

CUT
2

SEAM LINE

Topsy-Turvy Doll: pattern for doll body
(Enlarge 105 percent)

Figure-8 Stitch

Running Stitch

the back of the doll's head at the top (the dots on the pattern indicate the hair placement). Finish the hair of both dolls by fuzzing up the ends a bit. Demeter's hair is tied with a criss-crossed ribbon, as shown in the photo in the color insert.

Stuff all parts gently. Do not overstuff, especially the hands. Using button thread, use a figure-8 stitch (see illustration) to close the stuffing hole on the body. Fold the raw edges of the arms inside and stitch the ends closed with a simple running stitch, again using button thread. Don't clip off the thread when you get to the end of the arm, simply use it to whipstitch the arm tightly to the body where marked. Now use quilting thread to hand-stitch the fingers. To start the thread, make a single overhand knot in the end and plunge it inside about 1 inch away from where you want to start, wiggling the needle in the stuffing as you go. This will catch the knot in the stuffing and hold it inside the work invisibly. When you come out, make an extra little stitch and then hand-stitch the fingers. To end, take an extra little stitch, make a knot close to the fabric, and repeat the knot-catching process.

Witch Crafts

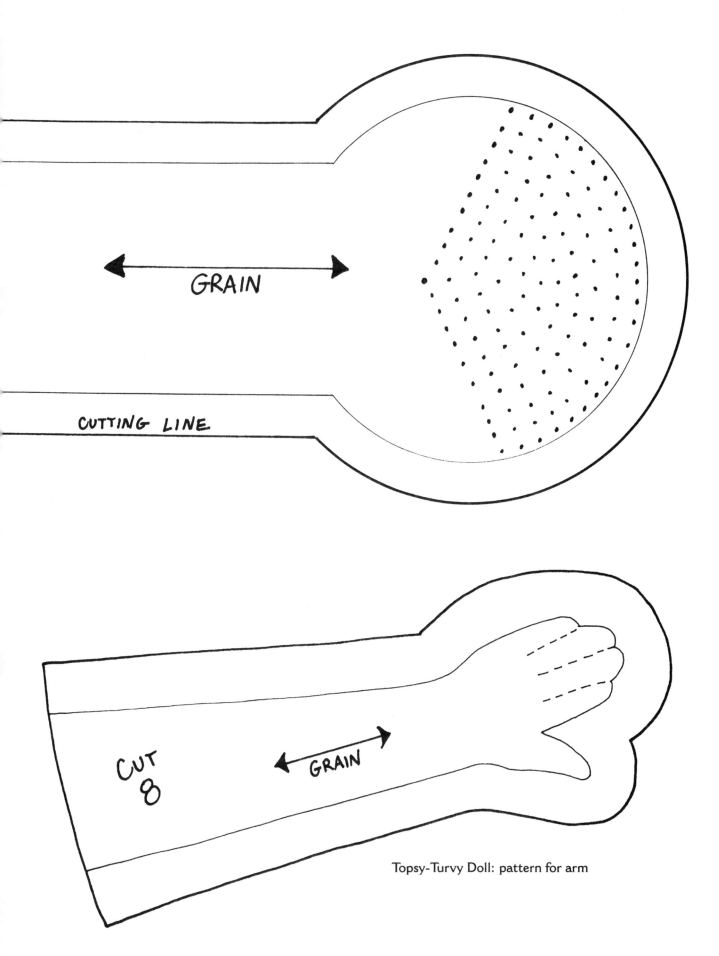

GRAIN

CUTTING LINE

CUT 8

GRAIN

Topsy-Turvy Doll: pattern for arm

The dresses of Demeter, Persephone, and Hades are identical. Cut a rectangle 18 inches by the fabric width for the underskirt and a 9-by-12-inch rectangle for the blouse. Fold the blouse fabric in quarters; mark a 3/4-by-1-inch curve at the center and cut to make the 1-1/2-by-2-inch oval neck opening. Fold under and stitch all raw edges, including the neck opening.

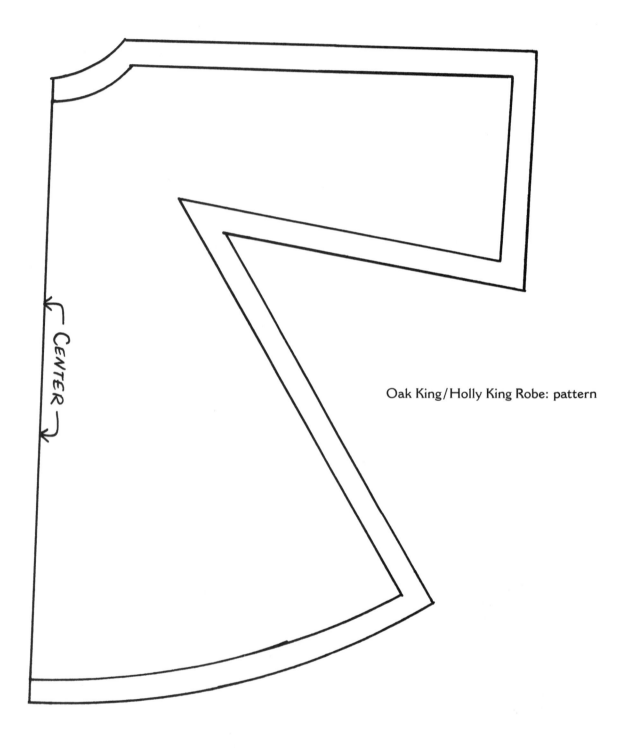

Oak King/Holly King Robe: pattern

Witch Crafts

Stitch the underskirt pieces along the long edge, right sides together, then stitch the short edges to make a tube. Turn right side out, place wrong sides together, and press hem. Run a basting stitch along the top raw edge, place over doll's head, and draw up gathers. Hand-sew the gathered edge to the waist of each doll, forming the two reversible skirts. Add a blouse to each doll, working the head carefully through the neck opening, gather and stitch at the shoulders, and tie with a ribbon at the waist to finish.

The Oak King and Holly King use the underskirt of the other dolls and have robes with sleeves that go over the underskirt instead of a Greek blouse. Cut one back and two fronts for the robe, stitch together, fold under, and stitch all raw edges. Gather and sew on the underskirt, this time attaching the gathered edge under the armpits rather than at the waist. Add the robe over this, and stitch the front closed if desired. (For illustration of finished Persephone/Demeter doll—both front and back views—see color-photo insert.)

Oak King's face

Holly King's face

Oak King with clothing

Cloak & Dagger Creations
61 Gilson Rd.
Littleton, MA 01460
(978) 486-4414
www.cloakmaker.com

Aside from their primary line of both historically accurate and fantasy clothing, this company carries beautiful metal cloak clasps as well as fabric trims in Celtic and tapestry styles.

Denver Fabrics
2777 W. Belleview
Denver, CO
(800) 996-6902
www.denverfabrics.com

Although they don't fill fabric orders due to limited staff, they do offer a large selection of trims, buttons, notions, patterns, cutting tools, and more.

Keepsake Quilting
Route 25B
P.O. Box 1618
Centre Harbor, NH 03226-1618
(800) 865-9458
www.keepsakequilting.com

This is a quilting catalog, but there are also loads of very unusual and interesting cotton prints (think seasonal, ethnic, animal prints, etc.), plus sterling customer service.

Sewing Supplies Warehouse
(630) 527-0386 (local)
(877) SEW-7400 (outside Chicago)
www.sewingsupplies.com

If you don't have a fabric store near you for some reason, try ordering your basic supplies here.

Reader's Digest Complete Guide to Sewing by Reader's Digest,
1995, ISBN 0888502478

This is one of those old-fashioned reference books that really does
tell you everything you need to know. Copious drawings assist the beginner along, whether your trouble area is hand sewing, alterations, threading up that machine, or understanding the basics.

Teach Yourself Cloth Dollmaking by Jodie Davis, Friedman/Fairfax
Publishing, 1995, ISBN 1567991599

If you've been inspired by the topsy-turvy dolls in this chapter, or if
you'd simply like a little more information on how to make fabric dolls,
this book is just what you're looking for.

4

EMBROIDERY

From the invention of thread forward, sacred embroidery has been used to inspire worshipers of all faiths. Perhaps the most exquisite surviving examples of early embroidery are found on ecclesiastical garments and altar pieces from medieval times. The embroidery techniques of these portraits and biblical scenes range from simple split stitch with wool yarn to couched metal threads painstakingly created from bars of real silver and gold.

There are hundreds of stitch variations, thousands of fibers to choose from, and an infinite number of ideas for what to embroider on a robe or altar cloth. Keep in mind, however, that all embroidery should be hand-washed only, preferably with a very mild soap designed for textiles. Some commercial laundry detergents and supposedly gentle lingerie soaps will make the colors of some embroidery threads run, so if you're not sure, it's better to be safe than ruin hours of hard work with one washing. Always test fibers you're unfamiliar with for colorfastness before starting your project.

TECHNIQUES FOR EVERYONE

I should warn you that embroidery is pretty addictive stuff for both men and women, so be prepared to catch the stitching bug! Even if you're a beginner, you probably at least know how to use an embroidery hoop and thread and needle. You might want to make a sampler as you go along and practice new stitches or techniques. This doesn't have to be anything fancy at all, just a scrap of fabric that you can use as a place to practice, and it will come in handy when you need to review how a particular stitch was done.

One of the easiest techniques, and one good for beginners, is counted cross-stitch. You simply make lots of little X's in different colors to form your design on special fabric. The fabric's weave has to be perfectly even and square so that the design isn't distorted when you work from a chart. Any craft store will have special fabrics made just for cross-stitch; they're known as aida, evenweave, linen, and other names. Best for beginners would be aida in 14 or 18 count (the number of stitches per inch), and this fabric is quite inexpensive and easy to find. There are also kits and pre-made items that feature aida cloth in a panel for you to stitch, like towels, tote bags, bibs, and so on. The charted designs are easy to follow, too, since each symbol represents a color of floss: It's somewhat like paint-by-numbers.

Needlepoint is perhaps next in difficulty and a little more expensive (but not much). You will need special needlepoint canvas, wool yarn, blunt tapestry needles, and an even hand. The only trick with needlepoint is to avoid distorting the canvas. You must select your stitches carefully and keep even tension on your stitches. Your finished product will be substantial and hard-wearing, like a cushion or seat cover, and so needlepoint is not usually used on clothing (unless it's an accent, like a border or pocket, or on heavier garments like vests and jackets).

Crewel embroidery requires some discipline and patience due to its free-form nature. Crewel is usually done on closely woven cotton or linen with thin wool yarn, although embroidery floss can also be used for a different look. Unlike cross-stitch and needlepoint, crewel uses many, many different stitches to achieve assorted textures and effects. Crewel is perfect for ritual clothing and other items as long as they are hand-washed so that the stitches don't become distorted.

Surface embroidery is much like crewel, but it expands into areas like metal thread work, embellishments like beads and sequins, and the extravagant 3-D stumpwork, where things literally pop out of the picture. These techniques are not recommended for clothing because they are difficult or impossible to wash, but they are stunning on altar cloths and other ritual items.

Here are some basic tips to make you a happier stitcher. Always begin stitching at or near the center of your design; it allows the fabric to shift around a little without distorting the stitchery, and in the case of charted designs, it's easier to find your place. Wash your hands before starting to stitch, and don't use hand lotion, which can leave discolorations or even oily spots on your materials. Use good lighting and a comfortable chair to prevent fatigue.

EMBROIDERY STITCHES

Back Stitch

Couching

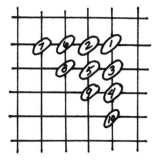

Basketweave Stitch

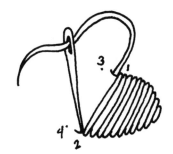

Satin Stitch

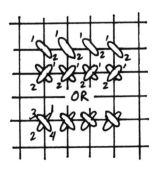

Cross Stitch

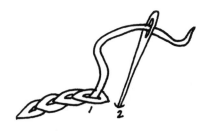

Split Stitch

Long and Short Stitch

Stem Stitch

To finish your needlework, either gently iron it, if it's not washable, or hand-wash it gently in the sink with a tiny bit of quilt soap (available at quilting or craft shops); then block your work. Needlepoint always needs the most blocking since the canvas will turn out distorted: Pin or staple your work to a sturdy frame and allow it to dry, correcting any distortion as needed. Other washed embroideries can simply be pressed with a warm (not hot!) iron on the back side while still damp, using a folded towel underneath if there is a lot of raised work, beads, mirrors, or other "lumpy stuff." If using synthetic fibers, test a scrap fiber with the iron before proceeding so you don't accidentally melt all your hard work. When it's dry, you're ready to frame your needlework or store it for later. If you store it, roll it carefully onto a cardboard tube or other similar shape. Folding needlework will at the least leave creases that will need to be ironed out, and at the worst could ruin it completely, as in the case of velvet or real metal threads that cannot be "unfolded" once stored this way.

THE PROJECTS

CROSS-STITCH WHEEL-OF-LIFE POUCH

This pouch can be created with a premade sachet pouch available in most craft stores, or you can easily make one with aida cloth using the pouch project in the sewing chapter. I've given two color variations here, one with a "neo-Pagan" color scheme and the other with a "sacred hoop of nations" color scheme. The patterns are virtually the same.

Cross-Stitch Wheel-of-Life Pouch (*made by Denise Rogers*)

YOU'LL NEED:

1 premade sachet pouch or a 5-by-10-inch piece of aida cloth, any color

2 straight pins

1 skein embroidery floss in each of the following colors:

For a neo-pagan wheel: Black, white, yellow, red, blue, green

For a sacred hoop: Brown, yellow, red, black, white

#5 embroidery needles

1 yard thin red cord (or, if using a premade pouch, 12 inches red or white ribbon)

Witch Crafts

Find the exact center of your stitching area; if you are using a pre-made pouch, this will be the roughly square area under the place where the pouch is tied shut with ribbon (look at the picture on the package). Use two crossed straight pins to mark the center before you start. Begin stitching the wheel (either the neo-Pagan or the sacred hoop) from the center, following the charts provided. When finished, tie closed with the cord or ribbon.

Stitch Count:	35 H × 35 W
Cloth Count:	14
Fabric:	Pre-made pouch, white
Design Size:	2.5″ H × 2.5″ W

Color Key

Symbol	DMC	Strands	Description
■	310	2	Black
•	702	2	Kelly Green
+	995	2	Electric Blue—dark
⁄⁄	666	2	Christmas Red—bright
·	743	2	Yellow—medium
W	White	2	White

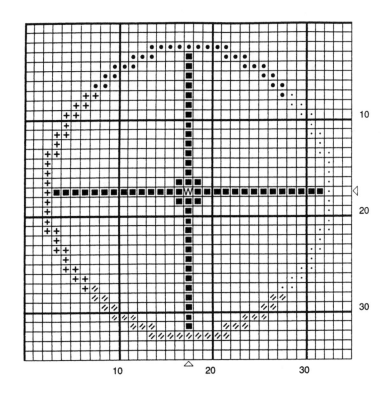

Neo-Pagan Wheel: color key and chart

Stitch Count:	35 H × 35 W
Cloth Count:	14
Fabric:	18 count sage green aida
Design Size:	2.5″ H × 2.5″ W

Color Key

Symbol	DMC	Strands	Description
■	310	2	Black
⁄⁄	666	2	Christmas Red—bright
·	743	2	Yellow—medium
▲	300	2	Mahogany—very dark
W	White	2	White

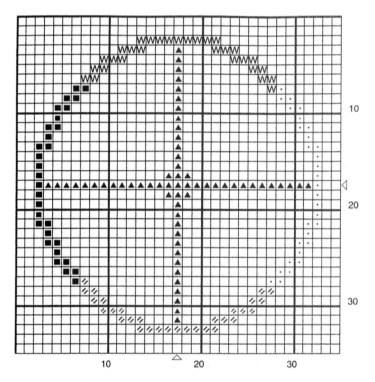

Sacred Hoop: color key and chart

CROSS-STITCH GREEN MAN SWEATSHIRT

What a fun way to celebrate the God! This project uses waste canvas to stitch his image on a sweatshirt, and you can play with the color palette to make a light-green springtime or multihued autumnal Green Man. Think of all the places you'll enjoy wearing this playful shirt. (Waste canvas is a special stiff, open canvas held together by starch, and it can be found at most craft stores that carry cross-stitch supplies.)

YOU'LL NEED:

1 sweatshirt (any size) in ivory, beige, pale green, brown, or black

1 8-by-10-inch piece 14-count waste canvas (if using an XL shirt or larger, use 2 overlapped pieces of 12-count, or even 10-count)

Needle and thread for basting

DMC floss (1 skein each):

> White
>
> 909 Emerald—very dark
>
> 905 Parrot Green—dark
>
> 733 Olive—medium
>
> 676 Old Gold—light
>
> 704 Chartreuse—bright
>
> 469 Avocado
>
> 310 Black

Small pliers or strong tweezers

Baste the waste canvas in the exact middle of your design area (see chart) allowing at least 1/2 inch of canvas past the edges of your design— more is better. Find the exact center of your actual stitching area by folding

---

Stitch Count: 92 H × 86 W
Cloth Count: 12
Fabric: Waste canvas on sweatshirt
Design Size: 7.67″ H × 7.17″ W

Color Key

Symbol	DMC	Strands	Description
·	White	3	White
▪	909	3	Emerald Green—very dark
●	905	3	Parrot Green—dark
+	733	3	Olive Green—medium
−	676	3	Old Gold—light
▽	704	3	Chartreuse—bright
▲	469	3	Avocado Green
B	310	3	Black

Backstitching

Around 733 leaves; 905 Parrot Green

Around bottom half of 733 leaves on face, around eyes and 469 leaves: 310 Black

Around 704 and 905 leaves: 909 Emerald Green

Green Man Sweatshirt: color key

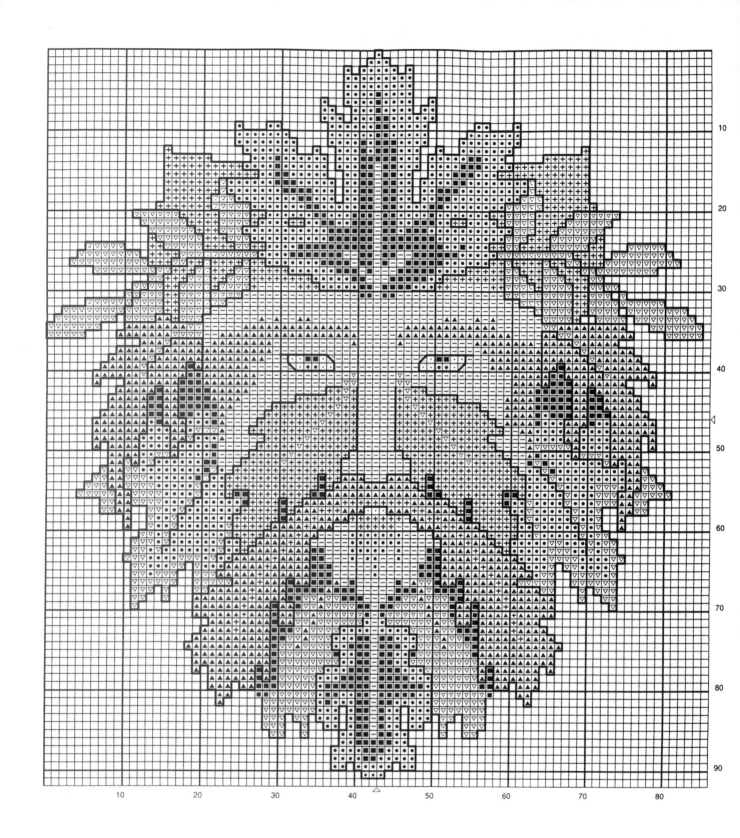

Green Man Sweatshirt: chart

the shirt into quarters, and mark the waste canvas. (It doesn't matter what you use to mark it since you'll be removing the waste canvas later.) Stitch the complete design using three strands of floss. Don't do any backstitching yet.

Wet the design area, wait a couple of minutes for the starch in the waste canvas to soften, and carefully pull out individual threads of the waste canvas with the pliers. Lay the piece flat to dry, then finish with the backstitching, using two strands of floss. (For illustration of finished project, see color-photo insert.)

CROSS-STITCH ELEMENTAL EDGING

Use these trims anywhere you'd like a strip of color, like the edge of an altar cloth, robe sleeves and hems, a guitar strap, or even as a choker or headband. To thread the metallics in the needle, pinch the end of the strand with your fingertips firmly and push the end carefully through your embroidery needle as you slowly open your fingertips. If this technique doesn't work for you, try putting a folded strip of paper halfway through the eye of the needle, inserting the end of the fiber through the paper loop, and pulling both through the eye.

You'll need:
   14-count 7/8-inch-wide Bucilla ribband in desired length
   Kreinik fine #8 metallic braid:
      028 Citron
      032 Pearl
      003 Red
      033 Blue (or 014 Sky Blue)
      009 Emerald (or 008 Green)
   #5 embroidery needles
   Freshwater pearl beads, extra small (optional, for Water only)

Each pattern has a "repeat," where the charted pattern ends and another section of the same pattern begins (see chart). In the case of the Earth border you can actually end between any of the leaves if you need to. If you are doing a project longer than the packaged ribband, you can either stitch another length onto the first and embroider through both thicknesses at the seam, or try calling your local needlework shop to see if it has longer rolls that can be cut to the length you need. If you are stitching lengths together, be sure to start the repeat at the seam to avoid gaps in your design.

Check your fibers for colorfastness before starting, especially if you substitute brands—some metallics can bleed when wet. Stitch the designs

Stitch Count:	60 H × 62 W
Cloth Count:	14
Fabric:	Ecru Bucilla Ribband
Design Size:	4.29″ H × 4.43″ W

Color Key

Symbol	Kreinik Fine #8 Metallic Braid	Strands	Description
+	033 or 014	1	Blue or Sky Blue
•	009 or 008	1	Emerald or Green
▲	003	1	Red
★	028	1	Citron
=	032	1	Pearl

Cross-Stitch
Elemental Edging:
color key and chart

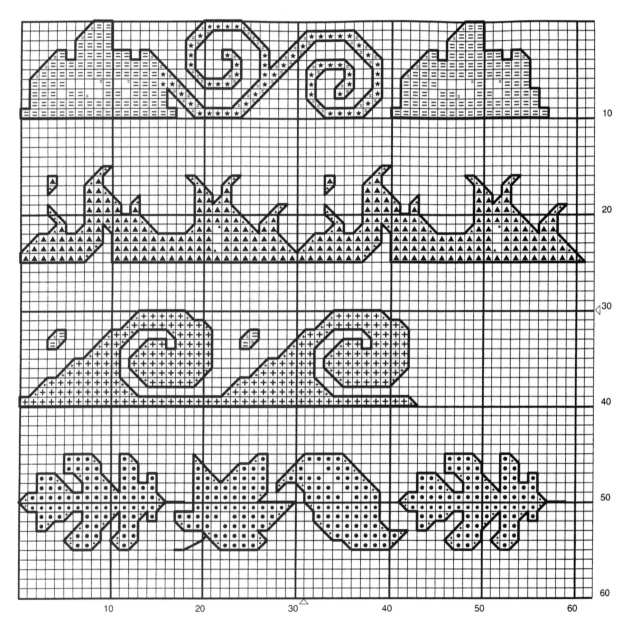

with two strands, backstitch with one strand. If you prefer, omit the pearl stitches on the Water border, and in the same place on the pattern attach real freshwater pearl beads. Hand-wash, dry between towels, then iron the borders facedown while they're still damp to correct any distortion. Iron on top of a towel if you used pearl beads. (For illustration of finished project, see color-photo insert.)

NEEDLEPOINT WINGED-SCARAB CUSHION

This design is an adaptation of the winged scarab pectoral found within Tutankhamen's mummy wrappings. The scarab represents transformation as it rolls the sun disc across the sky, and the ankh symbolizes "life." The cushion is perfect for events with limited or no seating. If you really love the design you might even want to frame the canvas instead of making it into a cushion. Use different gauges of canvas to create different sizes for the cushion. Recycled clothing or upholstery fabrics can be used for the sides and bottom if they're in good, strong condition.

YOU'LL NEED:

18-by-18-inch piece 14-count needlepoint canvas

18-inch stretcher bars or a 24-inch scroll frame

Paternayan wool yarn:

      14 yards Black (#220)

      2 yards Navy (#570)

      48 yards Dark Ice Blue (#550)

      6 yards Blue / Green Variegated (#2)

      55 yards Caribbean (#592)

      36 yards Spice (#852)

      24 yards Christmas Red (#969)

      8 yards Dark Christmas Red (#967)

Kreinik metallics:

      44 yards #16 braid or 1/6-inch ribbon 002 Japan gold

      60 yards #4 very fine braid 002 Japan gold

      48 yards 205C Antique Gold cord (optional)

#20 blunt tapestry needles

Rubber needle grabber

Scissors

3/4 yard heavy denim, canvas, mattress ticking, corduroy, or upholstery fabric for backing

2 yards medium cord piping, black (optional)

12-by-4-inch round foam pillow form or piece of foam cut to size

Black button thread and sewing needle

Stitch Count: 196 H × 196 W
Cloth Count: 14
Fabric: Mono canvas
Design Size: 14" H × 14" W

Color Key

Symbol	Paternayan	Strands	Description
■	220	2	Black
▲	570 / 550	2	Navy / Ice blend
•	550 + 205C	2	Ice + blending filament
☆		1	Kreinik #16 braid
#	02	2	Teal Varigated
/	592	2	Caribbean
_	852	2	Spice
+	969	2	Christmas Red
⁄⁄	852 / 969	2	Spice / Red blend
	967	2	Red dark
◔	969 / 967	2	Red / Red dark blend
⬚	967 / 220	2	Red dark / Black blend

Blends use one strand of each color in the same needle

Needlepoint Winged-Scarab Cushion: color key

Staple the canvas to stretcher bars or secure it well in the scroll-type needlework frame. You will be stitching with two strands of yarn cut to approximately 18-inch lengths. Use the metallics as they come off the spool. If you are using a different canvas count, adjust the number of strands and yardage accordingly.

Beginning in the center, stitch the design (see charts) using basketweave stitch when possible to minimize distortion. The Antique Gold cord 205C is used in the same needle with the Dark Ice Blue to add the hint of shimmer that real lapis lazuli has—if you are not an experienced stitcher or you are having a lot of trouble with the cord, feel free to leave it out. Work the variegated stitches as randomly as possible to re-create the speckled effect of the original pectoral's inlay work. For the blended sections, use one strand of each color specified and thread them together in the needle to make the area appear randomly speckled. Do all backstitching last, and remove your work from the frame.

Wash and block the needlework. When it's dry, trim around the stitching leaving 1 inch of bare canvas. Cut a circle the same size from your backing fabric and a strip 4 inches wide, with the length determined by the circumference of your circles. Stitch the strip to the needlework circle, then stitch the strip ends closed so that it forms a hoop. Overlap the

Witch Crafts

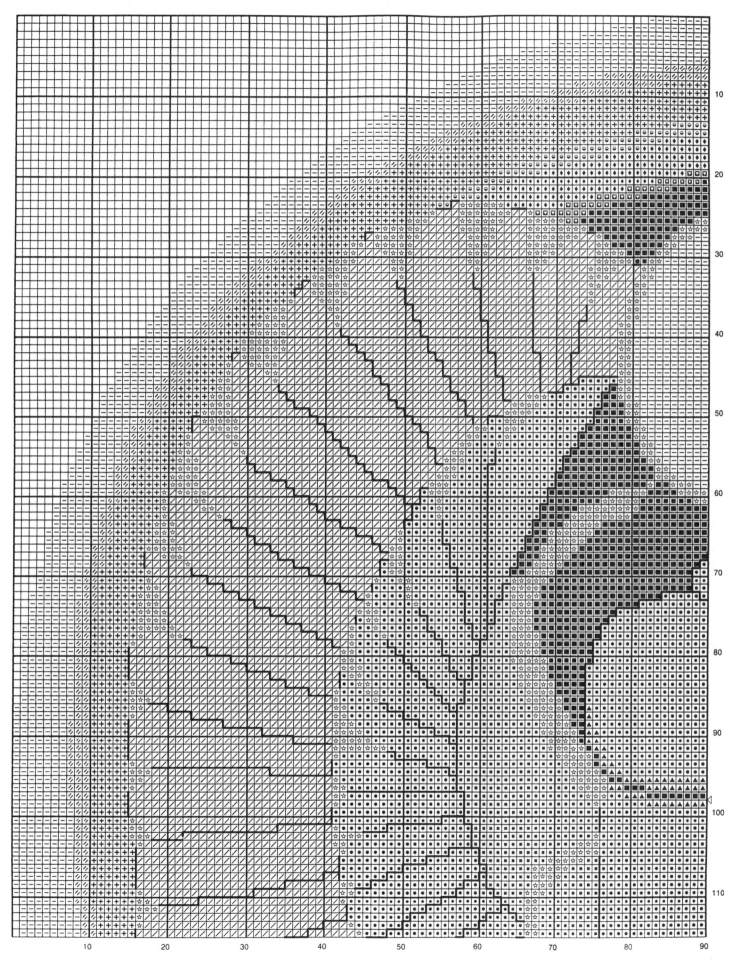

Needlepoint Winged-Scarab Cushion: chart (upper left)

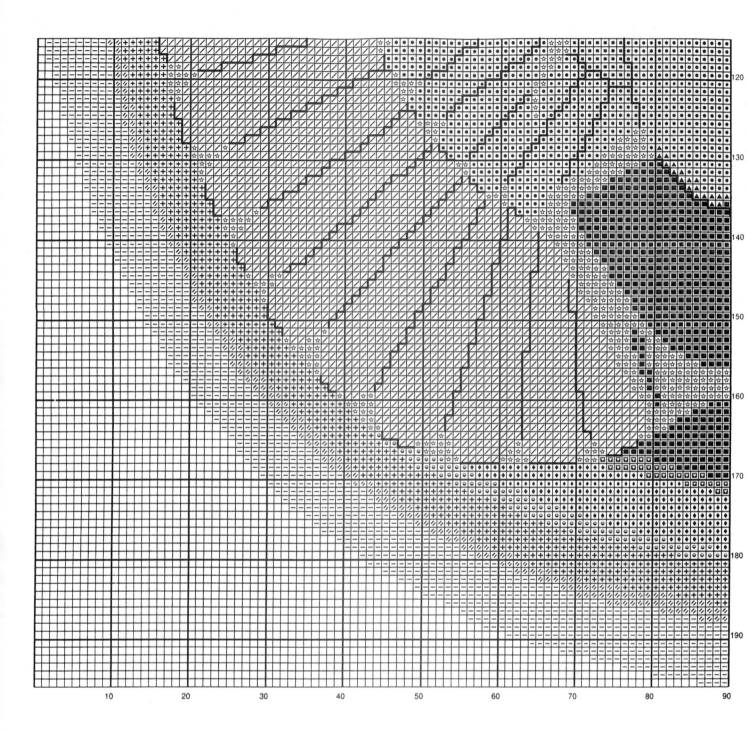

Needlepoint Winged-Scarab Cushion: chart (lower left)

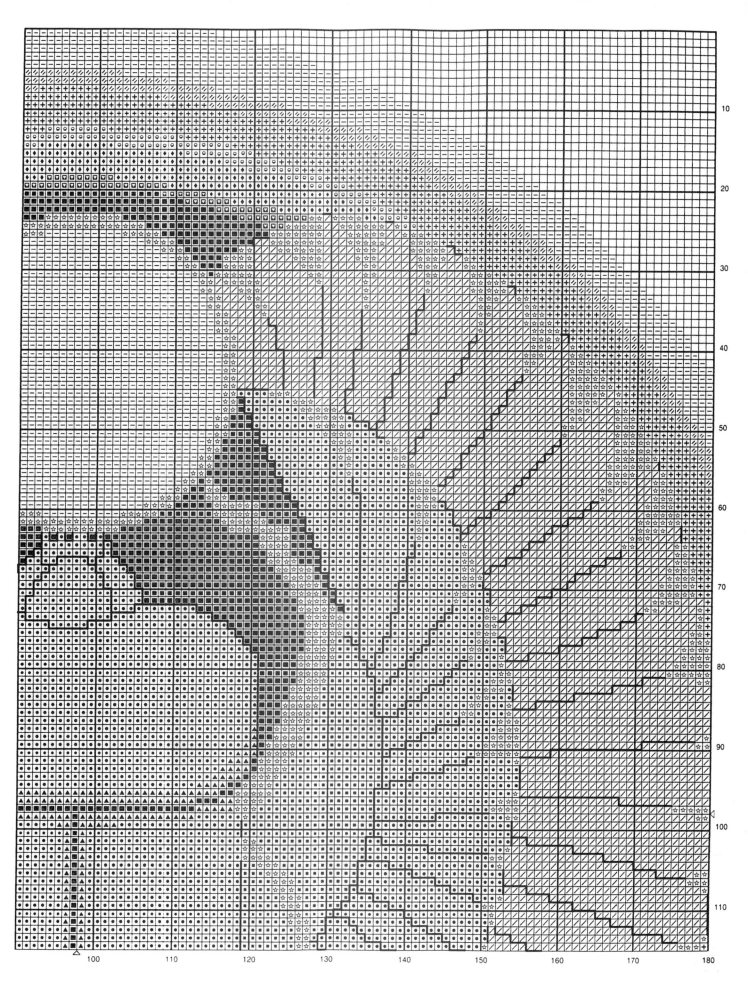

Needlepoint Winged-Scarab Cushion: chart (upper right)

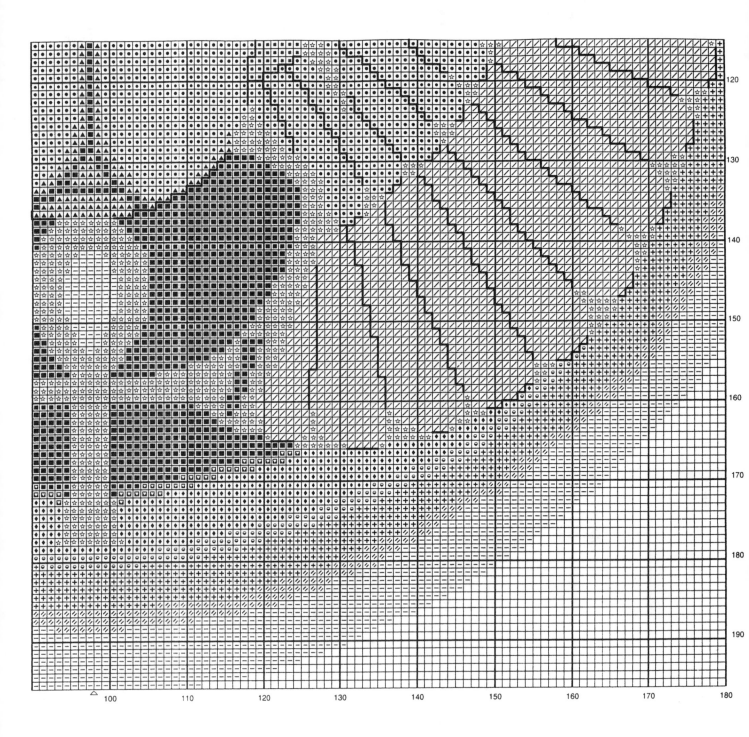

Needlepoint Winged-Scarab Cushion: chart (lower right)

stitched area by one or two stitches when adding the side strip (this avoids areas of blank canvas at the seams) and add piping in the seam for strength. Stitch the backing fabric circle onto the strip, leaving a 6-inch opening, and then secure the ends of the stitching well. Insert the foam pillow form; then hand-stitch the opening closed with button thread using the figure-8 stitch.

TRISKELLION APPLIQUÉ MEDALLION

This needlework technique dates from medieval times, when professional embroiderers stitched free-form designs onto linen, then cut them out to use on ecclesiastical robes. The triskellion (or triskelle) medallion has an almost endless number of different applications on garments, altar cloths, bags, almost anything you can think of to stitch it to. I like the asymmetrical "primitive" look of this particular pattern. Make more than one and play with the color combinations.

YOU'LL NEED:

- 6-inch-square piece of broadcloth, linen, or other light-to-medium-weight fabric
- 1 skein each embroidery floss in any two colors of your choice

Trace the design (see illustration on this page) onto your fabric with a permanent pen or washable fabric marking pen: It doesn't really matter which you use because you'll be covering all lines with embroidery. Using split stitch, work from the center outward using four strands of floss and laying the stitches as close together as possible. Avoid starting a new thread with a knot; weave new threads into the back of your existing work. If you must use a knot, don't place it next to the edge, where it could be clipped off when cutting out the medallion. Follow the natural curves of the spirals with your rows of split stitch, making little spirals for the circle shapes and working toward the centers of larger shapes to fill them in. Make your rows as close together as possible for good, solid coverage, and use even overall stitch tension to avoid a "puckered" edge.

Triskellian Appliqué Medallion: pattern

Embroidery   61

When all stitching is complete, use a steam iron set on "hot" or "cotton," and iron the embroidery flat. (If you don't have a steam iron, use a mist bottle to dampen the fabric a little.) Carefully clip out the circle, leaving 1/4 inch of fabric all the way around. Fold this edge under and stitch the medallion securely to your item of choice using floss or a matching quilting thread; then finish it neatly by using split stitch around the outer edge in either color of floss used for the triskellion.

GREEN MAN AND POMEGRANATE RUNNER

This runner, based on medieval motifs, won first prize in the embroidery division at my local county fair and a West Kingdom award from the Society for Creative Anachronism, a medieval reenactment society. It's stitched on pure Irish linen and features red glass beads to simulate pomegranate seeds bursting forth from the womb of the Lady while the Lord presides over your feast. Make it whatever length you choose. I made this one to fit my antique sideboard.

YOU'LL NEED:

>   2 yards white linen
>   #5 and #10 embroidery needles
>   DMC floss (1 skein each):
>> 815 Garnet—medium
>> 309 Rose—deep
>> 433 Brown—medium
>> 319 Pistachio—very dark
>> 320 Pistachio—medium
>> 935 Avocado—very dark
>> 937 Avocado—medium
>> 469 Avocado
>> 907 Parrot—light
>   Kreinik 002J #1 Japan gold cord (1 bobbin)
>   50 #8 clear red glass beads (approx.)

Wash, dry, and iron the linen, then cut a piece 12 inches wide and as long as needed. Turn under all edges and stitch; then use three strands of 815 to hide the stitching with a stem stitch all the way around the runner. (All stitches use three strands of floss and a #5 needle unless otherwise noted.)

Transfer the pattern (see illustration) onto both ends of the runner using graphite paper or a fine-tipped washable fabric pen. Stitch the stems with 433 in split stitch. Beginning in the center of the face, stitch the Green Man (except ferns) in 935, 937, 469, and 907 in long and short

stitch. Stitch the eyes with two strands 002J gold in horizontal satin stitch. Stem stitch face details with 935 as shown on pattern.

Green Man Runner: pattern

Stitch fern stems with 469 in split stitch, then stitch fern leaves with 907 in satin stitch, being careful not to pull too tightly to avoid puckering. Stitch scrolled leaves on brown stem with 319 and 320 in satin stitch. With the same colors, use stem stitch to outline the leaves, using 319 in the center. Stitch pomegranate centers with 815 in satin stitch, outsides of pomegranate with 309 in split stitch. Add red beads to center of pomegranates with one strand 815 and a #10 needle. Cluster the beads close together so they cover the satin stitching completely. Hand-wash to remove pattern marks and block until dry. (For illustration of finished project, see color-photo insert.)

METAL-THREAD PHOENIX PANEL

Like the triskellion medallion above, this spectacular panel can be finished separately, then stitched onto another piece of fabric. The design, representing the return of Wicca from the ashes of the Burning Times, is ideal for the back of a black ritual robe. Those with long hair might wish to place this panel on the front of a robe. Of course, you can also simply

frame and admire your stitchery, perhaps hanging this symbol of rebirth, power, and change over your altar.

YOU'LL NEED:

22-by-26-inch piece of medium-weight black velvet, denim, or other heavy black fabric

20-by-24-inch stretcher bars or picture frame

Kreinik Embroidery Color Effects, Energy (gold) Collection (includes gold ribbon)

#1 or larger and #10 embroidery needles, beading needle

1 skein black embroidery floss

Kreinik 1/8-inch Ribbon 021HL Copper Hi-Luster

Black seed beads

Black fusible interfacing (if applying to clothing)

Black sew-on hook-and-loop tape (if applying to otherwise washable clothing)

Secure the velvet to the stretcher bars tightly using a staple gun or tacks. Cut the acid-free tissue paper, provided with the Kreinik Energy Collection, in half. Set aside one half and iron the other half; then trace the phoenix design (see illustration) onto it with a permanent pen. Baste the design paper onto the velvet by hand with large basting stitches and heavy thread to avoid leaving a border of crushed velvet fibers around your finished design.

Metal-Thread Phoenix Panel

Kreinik Color Key

Eye, beak and claws: 002J-Japan
Eye feathers and tongue: 212-1/6" Ribbon
Wing feathers: 1800-Ombre
Inner edge of wing: 002-1/8" Braid
Breastbone: Facets
Feet: 102-#4 Very Fine Braid
Outline of phoenix: 202 HL-#16 Medium Braid
Pentacle: 021 HL-1/8" Ribbon
Pentacle outline: Torsade
Flames: 221-#16 Medium Braid

Metal-Thread Phoenix Panel: color chart

(Opposite) Metal-Thread Phoenix Panel: pattern
(Enlarge 155 percent)

Begin near the center of the fabric and start on lines that are "further back" in the image (the wings are behind the flames, which are behind the pentacle, which is behind the claws, etc.). Use the large needle to carefully draw a metallic fiber through to the front of the work; then couch it down every 1/8" or so with one strand of black floss until the end of a line is reached. The stitches need to be closer together on curves and may be up to 1/2" apart on straight sections. For very sharp corners, carefully fold the metal fiber back on itself and stitch down securely. The gold and copper 1/8-inch ribbons are tacked in the center with tiny stitches rather than couched down across their widths. Work the facets section last since the floss might catch in it and pull it out of place.

When all stitching is finished, add a single black seed bead to the center of the eye. Carefully tear away the tissue paper, using a needle and tweezers to help pick it out from behind the needlework. Now you can either leave the phoenix on the stretcher bars and frame it as is, or you can use black fusible interfacing to stabilize your stitching. Cut a piece to fit inside the stretcher bars; then iron it carefully to the back, testing the temperature of the iron on scrap fibers to make sure you don't melt the synthetic metallic fibers. When cool, remove the velvet from the stretcher bars, fold the raw edges back, and stitch around within 1/4 inch of the edge. Iron on another piece of fusible interfacing cut 1/2-inch smaller than the stitched rectangle; then add at least 6 squares of hook-and-loop tape so that the panel can be removed from your robe for washing. Omit the tape if your phoenix is to be applied to a jacket, banner, or other non-washable article, and attach it directly.

RESOURCES

Deb's Stitchery Store
401A East Arch St., Unit A
Madisonville, KY 42431
(270) 825-1237
www.debstitchery.com

This shop offers fabrics and fibers for charted designs (primarily needlepoint and cross-stitch). They have some unusual hand-dyed fibers as well as Mill Hill beads and printed charts.

Herrschners, Inc.
2800 Hoover Rd.
Stevens Point, WI 54492-0001
(800) 441-0838
www.herrschners.com

In the business of needlecrafts since 1899, Herrschners offers mail-order supplies for linens, needlepoint, cross-stitch, latch hook, afghans, and other crafts.

Kreinik Mfg. Co., Inc.
3106 Timanus Lane, #101
Baltimore, MD 21244
(800) 537-2166
www.kreinik.com

This maker of a galaxy of metallic and silk embroidery fibers is wholesale only, but it offers a toll-free consumer information line, and its Web site features a shop locator so you can buy locally. They are truly nice folks and will give you all the information you need on how to use their fibers.

Lacis
3163 Adeline St.
Berkeley, CA 94703
(510) 843-7178
www.lacis.com

Lacis offers all manner of esoteric supplies and books related to embroidery, lace, and bridal and historic reproduction needlework.

Complete Guide to Needlework by Reader's Digest, 1979,
    ISBN 0895770598

Here's an old standby filled with information that never really goes out of date. The people or projects may look out of fashion, but the basic information found here is timeless. It's a comprehensive resource no beginning stitcher should be without.

Cross Stitch for the First Time by Donna Kooler, Sterling
    Publications, 2000, ISBN 0806919639

The owner of Kooler Design Studios has put together a book for the person who has always wanted to try cross-stitch, but has no idea where to begin. From aida cloth to waste canvas, all your questions will be answered here.

Donna Kooler's Encyclopedia of Needlework by Donna Kooler,
    Leisure Arts, 2000, ISBN 1574861840

Tons of photos and lucid text set this book apart from others of similar title. Kooler has created a valuable book for those just starting out in needlework techniques such as needlepoint, cross-stitch, blackwork, silk ribbon, and more.

5

QUILTING

Quilting, the process of sewing layers of fabric together to make a padded blanket, has been around for centuries. What we usually think of when we imagine a quilt is pieces of many colorful fabrics sewn together, but this process (known as piecing or patchwork) is a relative latecomer, having been started in the late eighteenth century by thrifty American colonial housewives. Other pieced fabrics, such as African Kente cloth, have much earlier origins, but they were not created to be the top layers of quilted blankets such as the ones described here. The American pieced quilt really came into fashion during the middle of the nineteenth century and has enjoyed several revivals since then.

Quilts might not at first glance seem particularly Pagan, but many traditional pieced designs reflect the natural world that surrounded our ancestors, with names such as Bear's Paw, Maple Leaf, Harvest Sun, Garden of Eden, Lady of the Lake, and so many more, including more naturalistic plants and animals and some embroidered or appliquéd examples.

Of course, the modern quilter has at his or her disposal an incredible universe of fabrics to choose from, the latest equipment, and design techniques that have been developed in the last few decades. Gone are the days of scrimping every last bit out of the patterned cloth obtained from an empty flour sack. Today, if you want silver snowflakes, ruddy roosters, tiny faeries, or even a realistically rendered brick wall in fabric, all you have to do is go down to your local quilt shop or hop on the Internet. Reproductions of historic fabrics are also available for the traditionalist (like me). Unless you're working on a specialty item like a sateen wholecloth quilt or a velvet crazy quilt, always use 100 percent cotton fabric for both durability and even shrinkage when laundering. Always wash your new fabric to ensure colorfastness, and dry on the hottest setting for maximum preshrinkage.

A quick note about rotary cutters: I love mine! It makes cutting the pieces quick, easy, and precise, and I think it's easier on the hands than scissors. I have a Fiskars ergonomic cutter, and it's very comfortable and easy to use (the ergonomic ones are a little more expensive but well worth it). Get as large a cutting mat as you can afford, a straightedge for cutting long strips, and a blade sharpener, and you're ready to go. These tools are, of course, optional—but I highly recommend them. Make your own templates for any quilt block by cutting heavy cardboard to the right shape and size: You'll not only cut your pieces much faster, you'll have a durable block pattern forever.

QUILTING MAKES A QUILT

The word *quilting* actually refers to the process of sewing the layers together or to the stitches that accomplish this. Again, many traditional quilting designs are based on the beauty of the natural world—some popular ones include feather plumes, fern fronds, pumpkin seeds, spider webs, laurel leaves, ropes, geometric shapes, and really just about anything the quilter wants to fill in space with.

This chapter features eight Pagan quilting designs: Spider Web, for Grandmother Spider or just that Samhain look; Pentacle; Wheel of the Year, with its eight spokes; Laurel Leaf, reminiscent of the Greek tree of Apollo; and the four elements: Air, Fire, Water, and Earth. Resize these motifs as needed for your own projects. Spider Web, Pentacle, and Wheel of the Year are especially good for filling the blank spacer squares between pieced blocks, and Laurel Leaf can be made into a rope or vine to form a border motif.

WHERE TO BEGIN

If you're a beginner, it's best to start out with a simple pieced design that doesn't have any set-in corners (where you have to fit a piece inside a *V* shape) or too many small pieces that can throw off the symmetry of your whole design if the piecing is not executed skillfully. My first quilting effort was Bear Paw, and it was a good choice because it's rather forgiving, especially since you usually piece this quilt together with blank spacer blocks between the patchwork blocks. Another good way to start out is to do smaller baby quilts, as they will get you used to piecing while avoiding the

Spiderweb Quilting Motif

distortion problems that can occur with larger quilts. Precise stitching and piecing are essential to making a beautiful quilt. Some "slop" in piecing is fine when you're starting out on a simple quilt, but the more small pieces your quilt contains, the greater chance there is for distortion and complete frustration if your sewing is not right on the mark.

Appliqué quilts are not like patchwork piecing at all. With appliqué you are sewing smaller bits of fabric onto a full-size backing fabric that becomes the quilt top. In some cases this can be easier than patchwork

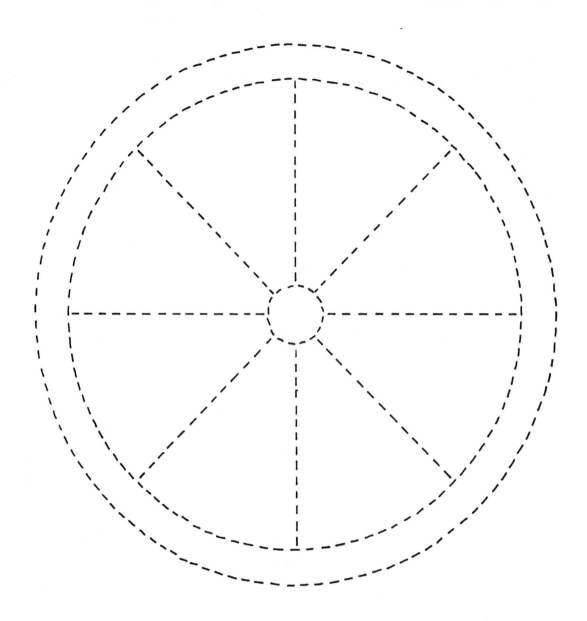

Wheel of the Year Quilting Motif

piecing, but if you're doing lots of curves and small shapes, it can get quite tricky, too. Start out with larger shapes and progress to smaller ones as you gain skill and confidence.

Once your quilt top is completed, you'll need to get some batting and fabric for the back of the quilt. For beginners, very thin batting is best because that will make stitching the layers together much easier, and synthetic batting is also easier to stitch through than natural cotton, which tends to "grab" the needle a bit. Carefully make a "sandwich" of your three layers; either roughly baste them together by hand (from the center out) or use lots and lots of safety pins to hold the layers together as you quilt.

Witch Crafts

Pentacle Quilting Motif

There are many ways of quilting and holding the "sandwich" taut. If you're in a hurry you can quilt by machine, but I prefer the simple meditative technique of hand-quilting. It's so relaxing to take a needle's worth of stitches as you follow the pattern and let your mind wander. It also puts far more of your personal energy into your quilt project. All you'll need for that is special hand-quilting thread (available at any fabric store), sewing needles, and a thimble.

"Betweens" are a popular needle size for quilters these days—they're a bit shorter than a regular sewing needle of the same diameter—but I prefer a longer needle and use a #10 or longer embroidery needle. It's a matter of personal preference, so experiment with different sizes and

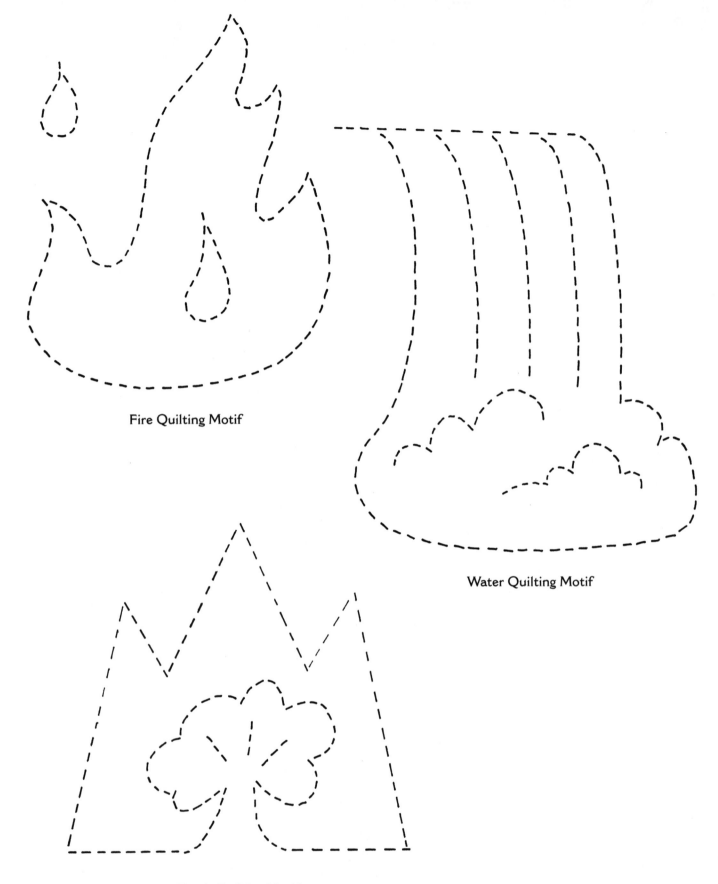

Fire Quilting Motif

Water Quilting Motif

Earth Quilting Motif

Witch Crafts

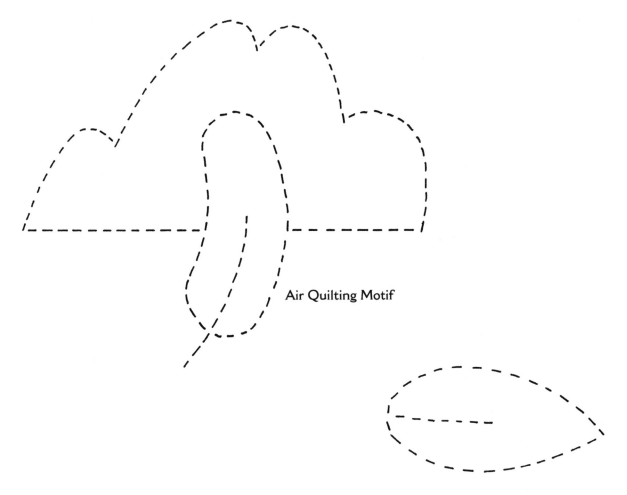

Air Quilting Motif

Laurel Leaf Quilting Motif

lengths to see what you like. A thimble protects your finger from the needle and is required at least on your top hand. I prefer not to use a thimble on my hand underneath the quilt because I have more control over the stitches that way, but again, it's purely personal preference. Thimbles can be traditional metal ones, snug-fitting leather ones, or special fabric ones, and there are even some specifically made for women with long fingernails (like me).

Quilt frames are almost as varied as quilters themselves. You can choose a large wooden hoop for lap quilting, PVC plastic "snap-on" frames for floor or lap, hardwood scrolling floor frames, and many more—plus variations of these. If you have limited space you'll need a foldable frame, or you can do like the pioneers did and store your quilt frame on hooks in the ceiling! For years my only frame was some 1-by-4-inch boards held together with C-clamps at the corners and balanced on the backs of two chairs. If your quilt frame doesn't hold the fabric on all four sides, such as a scrolling frame, you'll want to secure some fabric scraps around the open sides and tightly pin your quilt to these for proper tension.

To transfer the quilting design to your quilt, reproduce several copies of the pattern and run it through your sewing machine without thread, following all the lines. This will punch rows of holes where the stitching will go. Depending on whether you're quilting on dark or light fabric, pin the design in place and sprinkle chalk or graphite dust over the paper. You can make your own by shaving a graphite stick (available from art supply stores) or your child's sidewalk chalk with a sharp knife or scissor blade. Rub the powder through the holes and lift a corner to be sure the pattern has gone through to the fabric. When finished, you should have a clear image of your design laid out in little chalk or graphite dots on your quilt top (this will wash out easily). Make only about 12 to 18 inches ahead of where you're stitching or the design could rub away before you're finished.

Now you're ready to quilt. Make a single knot in your length of quilting thread and push the needle into the top layer and batting only a needle's length away from where you want to start. As you approach your starting point, wiggle the needle around in the batting so that the knot will be trapped inside. Come up at your starting point and pull the thread gently until the knot pops through the top and is caught in the batting. To end your thread, repeat the process; snip off the thread close to the fabric and work the end back inside with your fingernail.

I usually take about three stitches on the needle at a time, but you might work differently depending on the size of your needle. Practice will gain you smaller and more even stitches, as will thinner batting. Very thick batting might force you to use a stab-stitch rather than the quicker running stitch of most quilters. On very tight curves or tiny motifs you will probably want to use a stab-stitch.

THE PROJECTS

BEAR PAW QUILT

This was the first quilt I ever made, with the help of a friend of mine. The batting is so thick I had to stab-stitch the whole thing, and it took me over a year to complete. It's kept my family warm on many snowy nights in the mountains, the multihued bear paws keeping us safe and snug. While I enjoyed using scraps to make each block, you can use shades of brown, bear fabrics, or even fake fur to make up the paws. This pattern (see illustration) is for a twin or double bed.

Witch Crafts

YOU'LL NEED:

    5/8 yard scraps or purchased fabric(s) for the paws

    1 yard broadcloth for background

    1/8 yard for centers of squares (optional)

    1-1/2 yards for inner border

    2 yards for outer border

    2 yards for binding and back of quilt

    Batting, approximately 70 by 90 inches

    Curved quilter's basting safety pins

    Chalk or graphite powder

    Quilting needles

    Quilting thread

Cut out all pieces for the blocks, then begin piecing together the triangles for the paws. Wrong sides together, stitch the long sides of the triangles together (all seam allowances are 1/4 inch) and press open. To save time, chain-stitch the triangles (simply lift the presser foot when done with one pair of triangles, feed the next pair in, set down the presser foot, and continue). Clip the sets apart when you're done and press open the seams. Lay out the remaining block pieces and stitch them together in rows; then stitch the rows together to make the blocks.

When the blocks are all completed, spread a plain-colored sheet on your bed or the floor and lay out all the blocks "on point," as shown in the color photo. If you used assorted fabrics and made each block different, you'll need to fiddle with the arrangement of the blocks to get the most pleasing layout. Lay the plain blocks and triangles where they will go in the quilt and begin piecing. Start in the center and make long diagonal strips of blocks and triangles, pressing all the seams open when finished stitching. When all the strips are done, join them to complete the entire top, adding the top and bottom corner triangles last.

Make the inner border by cutting four 3-1/2-inch strips at least 7 inches longer than the overall finished size of the pieced blocks (two about 50 inches and two about 64 inches). Repeat for the outer border, making the strips 9 inches wide and 25 inches longer than the pieced blocks. (This accommodates the inner border as well.) Add the inner border by stitching all four sides to within 1/4 inch of the corners, then miter the corners by stitching at a 45-degree angle and trimming the excess. Repeat for the outer border.

Cut your backing fabric in half and stitch the two pieces together at the selvages to form a large rectangle. Press the center seam open, and don't worry about the raw edges for now. Make your "sandwich" by laying out the backing fabric right side down, then center the batting on it, then center your pieced top right side up and baste the whole thing together.

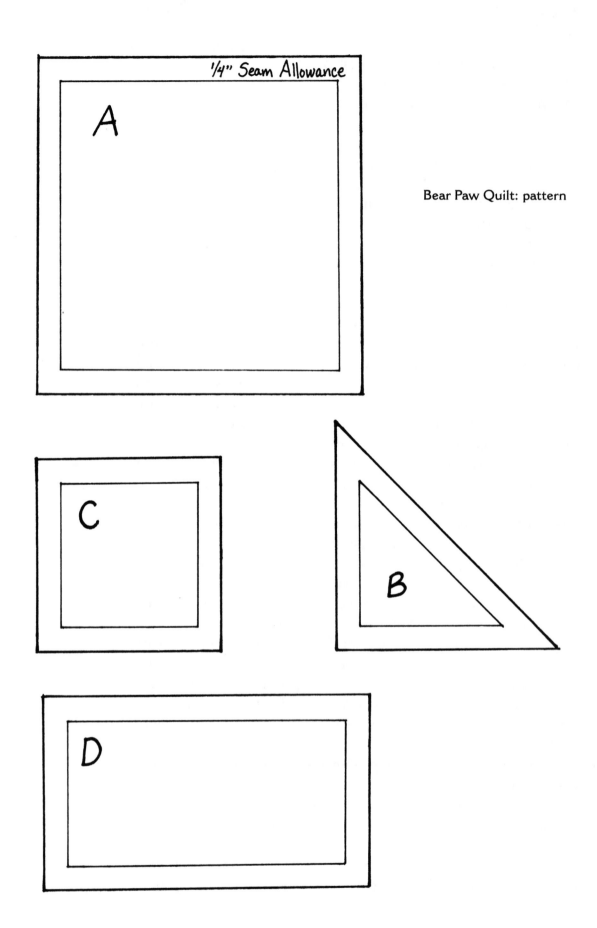

¼" Seam Allowance

A

Bear Paw Quilt: pattern

C

B

D

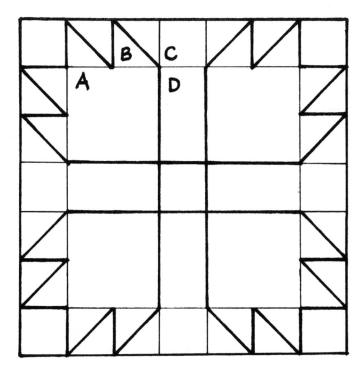

Place in a quilting frame or hoop and begin quilting from the center out. Use whatever quilting motifs you like, and remember to stitch no farther apart than about 3 to 4 inches or the batting could shift or clump up.

When all quilting is completed, trim excess batting evenly 1-1/2 inches larger than the quilt top all the way around, and trim the backing fabric 2 inches larger than the quilt top. Fold the edges of the backing around to the front of the quilt, folding the raw edge under 1/2 inch and pinning in place. Machine-topstitch the folded backing fabric edge 1/4 inch in from the edge of the quilt, or hand-stitch invisibly in place at the folded edge. At the corners, tuck any excess under to create a mitered corner to match the two borders, and stitch. (For illustration of finished project, see color-photo insert.)

HARVEST-SUN CRIB QUILT

This is a traditional Mennonite design that works well with scraps. I made this baby quilt (see color-photo insert) in honor of my nephew's birth. I envisioned the sun offering warmth and strength to him, and wanted to show that he was a ray of sunshine to his parents. Even five years later he sleeps under it at naptime at school, and it's one of his favorite possessions. Feel free to experiment with color combinations for a really radiant effect.

YOU'LL NEED:

- 1/4 yard red or burgundy small-scale print
- 1/4 yard solid yellow
- 1/4 yard brown medium-scale print
- 1-1/4 yards solid white or ecru (background and inner border)
- 1-1/4 yards solid red or burgundy (outer border)
- 1-1/4 yards solid yellow flannel (backing)
- 1 package 42-by-42-inch quilt batting
- Curved quilter's basting safety pins
- Chalk or graphite powder
- Quilting needles
- Quilting thread

Cut out your diamond shapes using the pattern pictured here. You will need 12 burgundy, 16 yellow, 16 brown and 28 white. Begin piecing the diamonds together in rows of three, until you have eight large pieced diamonds, each made from nine small diamonds. Stitch these large diamonds together, matching colors and seams, four at a time. Now stitch the two sets of four together along the straight center seam to make one large sunburst of eight pieced diamonds. Iron all seams open and as flat as possible.

Cut four white triangles and four white squares to fit. To begin setting the corner pieces, start on the inside of a V shape formed by two diamonds, placing the short side of a triangle on one of the straight sides and adjusting for the 1/4-inch seam allowance. Put the needle of your sewing machine down 1/4 inch in from the corner of the triangle and stitch to the edge. Now pivot the triangle so the other side of the triangle matches up with the next diamond and stitch. Lay flat and check for puck-

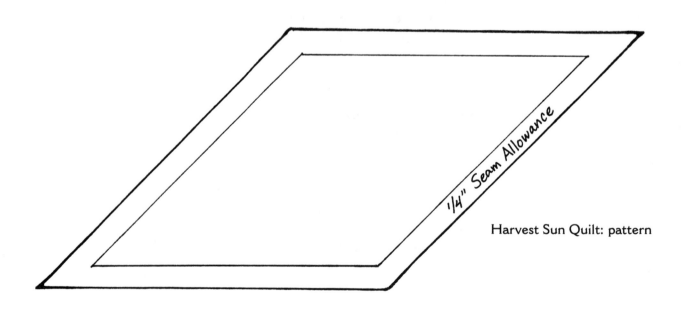

Harvest Sun Quilt: pattern

Witch Crafts

ering. The triangle should fit smoothly within the V. Continue setting in triangles and corner squares until the whole top forms one large square, as shown in the color photo.

Make a 2-1/2-inch-wide (includes seam allowances) white inner border and miter corners, as described in directions for the Bear Paw quilt (see page 77). Make a 3-inch-wide burgundy outer border in the same way. Baste the layers together, quilt as desired, fold the edge of the burgundy border to the back, and topstitch to make the binding and finish.

WATERCOLOR MOON AND ANTLERS WALLHANGING

This variation of the watercolor piecing technique uses low-contrast and monochromatic fabrics to paint an impressionist picture of a full moon in the night sky surrounded by antlers. Before I knew of their significance as the Goddess and her Horned God consort, I did some experimental photography and produced images much like the one this quilt is based on. Somehow my soul touched upon that ancient dance even if I didn't know it at the time.

You'll need:

1/4 yard assorted prints in each of the following colors:

White	Dark Blue
Very Light Gray	Medium Dark Blue
Light Gray	Medium Blue
Medium Dark Gray	Light Tan
Navy Blue	Ivory

1 yard Quilt-Fuse nonwoven fusible layout grid backing
Photo of the full moon
1-1/2 yards cotton fabric for back and binding

Use a minimum of two different print fabrics from each of the color categories (see chart), preferably more. Cotton sewing scraps are great for this if you have a lot saved up, and it's a fun excuse to go through your stash if you're an avid quilter. Cut the fabric into 2-inch squares, cutting more than you will need to complete the project. Don't worry about trying to categorize your fabrics too strictly, as this quilt looks best if the color values create a gradual transition, especially in the dark blues of the sky as they radiate out from the moon.

Cut the Quilt-Fuse into a square 40 inches (twenty marked squares) across and down, plus a few extra inches all the way around. If you happen to have a felt board wall, as some quilters do, pin up the fusible

Stitch Count: 22 H × 22 W
Fabric: Quilt
Design Size: 2.2″ H × 2.2″ W

Color Key

Symbol	Fabric Value Description
■	Medium Dark Gray
⬬	Ivory
·	Very Light Gray
=	Light Tan
•	Navy Blue
+	Dark Blue
▽	Light Gray
∩	Medium Dark Blue
−	Medium Blue
W	White

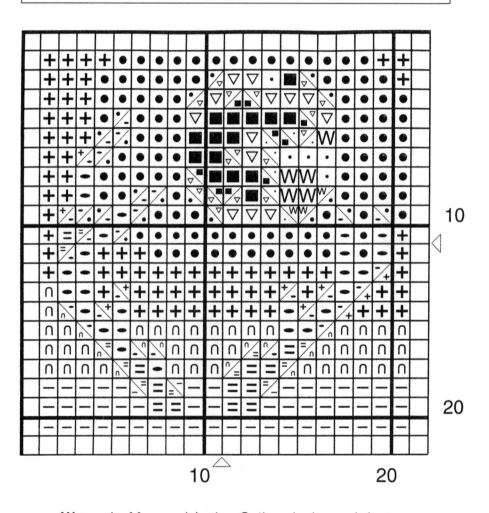

10

20

10   20

Watercolor Moon and Antlers Quilt: color key and chart

Embellished Novena (page 5)

Harvest Gel Candle (page 8)

Seaside Sand Candle (*made by Jen Snedeker*) (page 11)

Etched Votive Holder (page 177)

Sculpted Sabbat Pillar
(*made by Jen Snedeker*) (page 12)

Cross-Stitch
Elemental Edging
(page 53)

Watercolor Moon
and Antlers
Wallhanging (page 81)

Bear Paw Quilt (page 76)

Harvest-Sun Crib Quilt (page 79)

Cross-Stitch Green Man
Sweatshirt (page 50)

Green Man and Pomegranate Runner (page 62)

Persephone/Demeter Topsy-Turvy Doll—
front and back (page 37)

Basic Drawstring Pouches (page 30)

Simple Gathered Skirt (page 32)

Hoof and Horn Rattle
(page 107)

Seasonal Wreath (page 96)

Gourd Rattle (page 99)

Carved Staff (page 124)

Shaman Sage Staff (page 108)

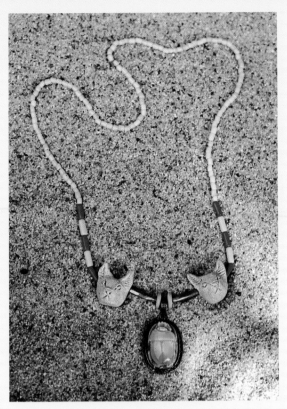

Polymer Clay Necklace (page 18)

Egyptian Collar (page 23)

God/Goddess Wire Circlet (*made by Mary Crawford*)
(page 20)

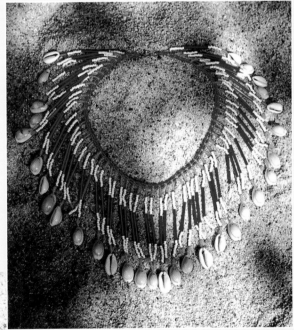

Beaded Cowrie Shell Choker (page 21)

Bottle Cap and Bead Sistrum (page 95)

Decoupage
Treasure Box
(page 130)

Crackle-Finish Divination Tray (page 145)

Papier-Mâché Star Box (page 140)

Oak-Leaf Candleholder
(page 150)

Yule Tree Ornaments (page 142)

Trompe l'Oeil Altar Top (page 151)

Pennsylvania Dutch Hex Sign
(page 143)

Festival Feast Bowl
(page 149)

Inspirational Collage
(page 129)

Cutwork Candleholders (*designed and made by Jen Snedeker*) (page 162)

Handmade Paper with Herbs (*made by Jen Snedeker*) (page 133)

Ancient-Mother Incense Burner (page 164)

Goddess Sculpture (page 160)

Tripod Incense Brazier (page 165)

Pricked Candle Lampshade
(page 135)

Quilted-Leather Book of Shadows
Cover (page 112)

Simulated Stained-Glass Mirror
(page 171)

Triple-Moon Suncatcher (page 170)

Mosaic Stepping-
Stone (page 174)

Scratchboard Suncatcher (page 173)

Tooled-Leather Green Man
Guitar Strap (page 113)

backing so that it hangs vertically; otherwise, spread a large towel on a flat surface that you will be able to leave undisturbed until you're done arranging the squares. Outside the design area on the Quilt-Fuse, mark the center points on the top and side with a sewing pencil or chalk.

Start with the moon and carefully lay out your cut squares according to the pattern values (see illustrations) and using the moon photograph as a shading reference. Press the fabric down firmly into the backing, especially if you have it pinned vertically. When the whole squares are in place, cut the extra gray and white pieces into half-squares, match the values, and stitch together. It's a good idea to put only a few sets together at a time to avoid confusion. Put these half-square sets in place and carefully iron all the moon pieces to the fusible backing according to the Quilt-Fuse directions. Avoid ironing beyond the edges of the moon pieces so that the backing will fuse to the sky pieces properly (and to keep your iron clean).

Next lay out the sky squares, moving from the very darkest navy next to the moon to the lightest navy/dark blue at the edge of the navy area. Finally, lay out the antler pieces and create the sky/antler half-squares as you did for the moon/sky pieces. Iron small areas as you progress to keep the pieces from shifting around—and even coming off if there's an errant wind or a curious cat.

When all the squares are secure, stitch the quilt. Fold on each dotted line as marked on the fusible backing, then stitch a 1/4-inch seam. When all seams of one direction are finished, press the quilt and stitch the seams in the other direction. Press when finished and lay flat.

Cut a piece for the backing that's about 2 inches larger than the top all the way around and lay the top in the center. Machine-stitch "in the ditch" between all the squares to secure the top to the backing. Fold up all the edges to make a neat border, folding the corners and raw edges under. Top-stitch in place 1/8 inch from the edge and at the corners. (For illustration of finished project, see color-photo insert.)

CELTIC PENTACLE BIAS-TAPE BANNER

Bias tape is cut on the diagonal, or bias, of the fabric, and since it's quite stretchy it eases around curves well. I've seen variations on this Celtic knotwork pentacle and thought the bias-tape appliqué technique of quilt-making would be perfect for the interlaced effect. You can use purchased tape for this project, but making your own ensures you have just the color and texture you want, plus it puts more of your energy into the finished banner. This would also make a great altar cloth, especially if sewn on a round background and used on a round table.

Celtic Pentacle Bias-Tape Banner: pattern

YOU'LL NEED:

Rotary cutter

1 yard ivory or light tan low-contrast print

Washable fabric pen, chalk, or dressmaker's pencil

36-inch metal straightedge or ruler

1/2-inch bias-tape maker

1/2 yard green low-contrast print

Iron and ironing board

Witch Crafts

Large towel
1 package 1/4-inch Steam-A-Seam 2 fusible tape
1/2 yard brown low-contrast print
Needle and thread to match the green and brown fabrics
Dowel

Cut the ivory fabric to measure 34 inches square and fold it in half, wrong sides together. Make a mark on the fold 3 inches down from the top and bottom, refold in the other direction, and repeat. Now measure 10 inches from each corner and mark. You should have eight marks forming a rough circle on the right side of the square. Position the straightedge exactly between each of these marks and measure up 4 inches from the edge, then mark. Now you should have a total of sixteen marks forming a circle.

Following the measurement given on the package of your bias-tape maker, and using the straightedge as a guide, cut several strips from your green fabric at a 45-degree angle to the grain. Go ahead and use most of the triangle you cut off from your first cut—you'll be using many shorter pieces in your design. Stitch enough of the strips together to make one long strip that's about 90 inches long. Follow the directions given for using the bias-tape maker, using a steam iron or misting the fabric with water if your iron has no steam setting. In addition to the one long strip, make five or six more bias strips. (You can always make more if you need them.)

Lay the towel down on a table near your ironing board and place the ivory fabric in the middle. Follow the marks and make a large circle with the fusible tape, pressing the stickier side firmly onto the fabric. (I found that the side clinging to the paper tended to be stickier.) When the circle is finished, begin at the top and press the green bias tape onto the fusible tape circle. When you reach the beginning again, clip the end of the bias strip 1/2 inch longer and fold it under, hiding the raw edge of the other end. Iron the circle down securely to the fusible tape, following the directions on the package.

At the inside top of the circle, make a mark. Measure 17-1/2 inches around the edge in both directions and make two more marks. Continue around and make two more marks, adjusting if necessary to make the marks evenly spaced. Now use the straightedge and draw lines to connect the marks and make a pentagram. Follow these lines with more fusible tape. Clip the end of a piece of bias tape to make an even edge and tuck it under the edge of the green circle at one of the marks: You may have to pull up a bit of where the tape under the green circle is fused to the background fabric. Stick the bias tape to the fusible tape as before. Break the line where necessary to overlap, and interweave the lines of the pentacle, tucking the raw edges under the overlapping lines. Iron down the lines securely.

Make several strips of brown bias tape just like you made the green bias tape. Follow the pattern provided (see illustration) and draw the knotwork designs between the points of the star as shown. The brown bias strips are always under the green and never overlap them. Take your time and place fusible tape where the knotwork lines will go. If you get confused as to which line goes over which, remember to ignore the green lines, it's always the same pattern for each knot, and the pattern alternates between over and under. (If the line in question went under the other line, at the next intersection it will go over the other line.) Stick the brown bias strips on the fusible tape a little at a time and iron firmly. Tuck under any raw ends, and iron to fold them. When all knotwork is ironed in place, trim and invisibly stitch down all raw ends, then invisibly stitch down all brown and green lines securely.

Fold under all raw edges of the ivory fabric and stitch. To hang, make a 2-by-34-inch tube from some scrap fabric, stitch it on the back, and place a dowel through the tube.

RESOURCES

Fabrics To Dye For
2 River Rd.
Pawcatuck, CT 06379
(860) 599-1588 or (888) 322-1319
www.coloursfromnature.com

If you're looking for beautiful hand-painted fabrics and many other quilting supplies, you'll find them here. The swirled, marbleized, and abstract fabrics also feature the metallic highlights so popular with today's quilters.

Ginger's Needleworks & Quilting
1001 East Gloria Switch Rd.
Lafayette, LA 70509-2047
(337) 232-7847
www.quiltknit.com

If you can't find that new, unusual, or novelty fabric you're looking for anywhere else, try Ginger's. She has an easy-to-use Web site that features quickly loading images of each print, and you can order offline if you prefer. And don't forget to check out her other supplies too.

Keepsake Quilting
Route 25B
P.O. Box 1618
Centre Harbor, NH 03226-1618
(800) 865-9458
www.keepsakequilting.com

Tons of interesting fabrics, books, tools, and tips for the quilter are to be found in this amazing catalog.

Piecework Fabrics
P.O. Box 443
Oneonta, NY 13820
(607) 431-9675
www.pieceworkcompany.com

This company is primarily a source of unusual cotton quilting fabrics, and their Web site is searchable by either designer or manufacturer. Notions, books, and gifts are rather limited in selection, but their terrific fabric prices make up for this deficit.

About.com's Quilting Section
http://quilting.about.com/hobbies/quilting/mbody.htm

On this Web site you'll find lots of great information, free block patterns, advice, instructions, and tips on where to shop on-line and locally. If you can't find something here, ask the site's expert guide.

Celtic Quilt Designs by Philomena Wiechec, Celtic Design Co., 1980, ISBN 0963198203

This older title can be somewhat hard to find, but Wiechec originated the idea of the bias-tape Celtic knot quilt. Her technique uses bias tubes rather than traditional bias-tape strips.

Celtic Quilts by Beth Ann Williams, Martingale & Co. Inc., 2000, ISBN 1564773108

Beautiful selections of modern fabrics make the designs in this book shine. There are lots of helpful tips to be found here, and she uses the fusible strips as an underpinning as I did in my Celtic Pentacle Bias-Tape Banner.

Quick Watercolor Quilts by Dina Pappas, Martingale & Co. Inc.,
    1999, ISBN 1564772705

Pappas uses the same "fuse, fold and stitch" method I used on my
Watercolor Moon & Antlers Wallhanging. Although her palette is pur-
posefully limited, this book will help you become more familiar with piecing a watercolor quilt and help you design your own.

Quilter's Complete Guide by Marianne Fons and Liz Porter,
    Oxmoor House, 2nd rev., 2001, ISBN 084872466

This book truly is a complete full-color guide for the quilter, especially for the beginner who needs detailed information on basic techniques,
materials, color selection, tools, and more. An absolute must if you're at all
serious about quilting.

6

FLORA

Flora is the Roman Goddess of flowers and springtime, but in modern terms *flora* has come to mean simply "plants," especially those in a particular area. What do you know about the flora in your area? Even city folks have access to wildflowers, trees, edible weeds, and cultured gardens. If you don't have room for a single pot of herbs on a windowsill, it's good for the soul to take a drive and enjoy a local park or, better yet, go camping and enjoy Flora on her own terms for a while.

The very first tools ever used were probably made from plants: Some birds use sticks to get at grubs hidden inside tree branches, and chimpanzees use blades of grass to extract a termite snack from tiny access holes in the nest. Baskets actually predate pottery as Stone Age containers; clothing and mats of plant fibers have been found all over the world; and plants play an important part in many religions, from the sacred lotus and papyrus of Egypt to the sacred white sage and peyote of the American Southwest. Herbs, of course, have been the backbone of human medicines from ancient times until today. As modern medicine rediscovers uses for plants like feverfew, willow, digitalis, and the tea tree, we have come full circle and return to our "roots."

The projects in this chapter include plants dried and green, wild and purchased, real and imitation. Whether serving as the handle of a rattle or the body of an incense potpourri, plants are vital and honored here. Without Flora, we could not walk the Pagan path.

WALK-IN-THE-WOODS DEVOTIONAL SCULPTURE

Treat this as a mini-ritual by purifying yourself before you start on your walk and communing with your Deity. Ask him/her to send you a sign or show you a path, then start walking. Don't be distracted by trying to go the "right" way, simply start walking. A good way to keep your mind receptive is to sing or chant (aloud or in your head) while you walk, but don't overly focus on the song. When you find a sign, you will know. This can be a feather, an acorn, an interesting leaf, a pretty stone, a fallen bird nest—whatever is meaningful to you. If you didn't find anything large to attach your smaller items to, don't forget to pick something up on your way back. Also remember to leave an offering of thanks for your gifts. This technique can also be used at the beach, in the desert, anywhere you like. My grandfather made a fascinating beach sculpture from a piece of driftwood that was covered with shells, stones, and even a coiled piece of rusty wire.

YOU'LL NEED:

Keen eyes and an open mind / heart
Bag or basket for carrying home your finds
Glue gun or quick-drying tacky craft glue
Picture-hanging hardware (optional)

Take your largest item (such as a pinecone, piece of wood, stone, etc.) and find the side or angle that pleases you most. Simply attach other

Walk-in-the-Woods Devotional Sculpture

found items to make a pattern, or place them randomly, or arrange them in a pyramid—there is no wrong way to make this sculpture. You'll know when you're done. If you used a flat piece of wood for your sculpture base, you can hang it on the wall instead of using it as a tabletop piece.

OUTDOOR ALTARS AND SHRINES

No matter whether you prefer Chaos or Zen, a little devotional grotto can be just what you need for a quiet moment of meditation. Leave an offering, add some plants, sing a hymn, or just gaze upon the beauty of nature in this sacred space you create yourself. All ingredients are optional—allow this project to be a springboard to what your heart tells you to make.

YOU'LL NEED:

> Stones, large or small
> A stump, weathered plank, or other flat surface
> Deity sculpture
> Plants (native wildflowers, herbs, roses, etc.)
> Small outdoor fountain (optional)

Find an out-of-the-way spot or hidden niche in your yard—a corner of your apartment balcony is fine, too. Stack the rocks on either side to make a base for the wood, or use a stump to hold a flat flagstone. Make the whole thing of stones or wood, whatever you like. The idea is to make a shelf for your deity image to sit up off the ground and a roof above to protect it. When you've finished the altar to your satisfaction, plant fragrant herbs and flowers around the sides.

EASY ALTAR BONSAI

It's not easy to keep a maple tree 12 inches tall for fifty years, but it is easy to start your own bonsai tree. The Japanese art of bonsai is an ancient one, and this relaxing hobby enables you to create the perfect tree or miniature grove from your mind's eye. A full-grown and well-cared-for bonsai tree can live indefinitely and can be a powerful centerpiece for an altar, especially when tree imagery is the focus of the ritual. I used a bonsai to represent the Tree of Life in one ritual, and it was the perfect anchor we needed that night. The bonsai pictured here was made especially for this book; I used a santolina herb with a small image of Ganesh nestled in the moss.

Easy Altar Bonsai

YOU'LL NEED:

1 baby shrub with small leaves, nursery
    stock or home-grown
1 bonsai pot (size depends on tree)
Moisture-retentive potting soil
Small pruning shears, clippers,
    or traditional bonsai shears
Smooth river pebbles, moss, moss
    spores, small figurine (optional)
Copper wire (optional)

Many wild and native shrubs work well as bonsai, so look around your yard for suitable material as well as the nursery. For the beginner, I recommend hardy, small-leafed plants like rosemary, wild huckleberry, boxwood, junipers, azalea, cedar, and so on. Look at a few books about bonsai or surf the Internet to get an idea of what shape you want. If you already have a plant you want to work with, choose the best form to suit that plant.

Let's assume you're starting with a 1-gallon juniper that is not root-bound (too many roots in the pot) and has an interesting trunk shape. Get a pot about 3 to 4 inches deep and about 8 inches wide that will complement the overall form and color of the plant. Remove the plant from the nursery pot and clear out most of the soil. You might need to clip away some of the roots or shorten long roots to fit them into the new pot. Pack the roots into the pot and begin working soil among them. Do not plant your tree in the middle of the pot: Traditional bonsai is always planted offset from the center, often about one-third the distance from the edge to the other side. Allow the soil to become slightly mounded under the trunk of the tree and press the edges down firmly. Water thoroughly and add more soil if necessary.

Now comes the part you've probably seen on television. Begin clipping away parts of the plant to create a perfect tree. A good way to do this is to hold the tree up to the light to get an idea of the silhouette, begin by removing any dead growth, and start pinching out any weak or undesirable stems. As the woody trunk is revealed and you get a clearer idea of where the tree's form is going, close your eyes for a moment and visualize a full-size tree similar to this one—perhaps a windswept Monterey cypress, a stately old oak, or a manzanita tree by a river. Continue clipping and pinching off foliage until you have created a miniature version of that perfect tree in your mind.

To finish off the completed look of a miniature wild tree, you can add some interesting stones or a small figurine and use moss spores (available by mail order or at some nurseries) to create a lush green carpet of "grass" under your tree. You can also use moss gathered from your backyard, pressing it firmly into place on top of the soil (that's what I usually do).

Unless created from indoor houseplants, all bonsai trees should be kept outdoors as much as possible. (Bring tender plants inside for the winter where necessary.) Only bring your bonsai tree indoors for a few days at a time for maximum health, and check to be sure it has enough water every day. If the soil is moist, it's okay, but if it's dry you will need to gently submerge the pot in a larger bowl of water until all air bubbles have been expelled. Fertilize sparingly in the summer, using a very dilute mixture: You're trying to keep the plant small, not encourage lots of growth.

As the tree matures, you may wish to use copper wire to make the supple branches conform to your vision. Secure the wire deep in the root ball, feeding a double length through halfway and then wrapping the two wires around the trunk and branches. You will then be able to bend the branches in a picturesque gnarled form without harming the tree. Keep pinching off any leaves you don't want, and keep on top of that water.

HERBAL TOPIARY

Herbal Topiary

We've all seen topiaries before, perhaps at a public garden park or even a theme park (although they usually aren't very healthy, if they are even real plants). Imagine having your own miniature one for a feast table display, or even a giant Goddess frolicking through your yard. The two extremes use the same principle, but the topiary described here is the tabletop version filled with moss for fast results.

YOU'LL NEED:

    Decorative pot, such as terra cotta, glazed ceramic, etc.
    Purchased wire form or 16-gauge wire to make your own
    Sphagnum moss
    Chicken wire
    Potting soil
    About 12 small-leafed dense plants of the same type,
        such as rosemary, boxwood, juniper, miniature ivy, etc.
        in six-packs or 4-inch pots
    Hairpins
    Wire cutters

Herbal Incense Potpourri

Begin this topiary well before you will need it, allowing plenty of time for the plant to grow and fill the topiary form (at least three months). Fill the form with sphagnum moss and pack it tightly inside. Cover the form with chicken wire if necessary to contain the moss. Fill the pot with soil and anchor the form securely in the soil so that it won't tip.

Wherever the form touches the soil, plant a single plant and use hairpins to secure it to the moss. (If there is no moss, use a twist-tie to secure the plant to the bare wire.) Plant more plants inside the moss-filled form, cutting holes in the chicken wire if needed. Secure with hairpins. Keep the moss moist by watering often, submerging the entire thing in a bucket if a watering can isn't doing the job. Keep the plants pruned close to the form, within about 1/2 to 1 inch of the wire, and encourage trailing plants to creep over the surface and take root.

Keep the topiary in a sunny window, rotating it every few days for even growth. Decorate with ribbons for table use.

HERBAL INCENSE POTPOURRI

In ancient times, incense originated from the burning of sweet-scented plant materials such as resins and dried fruits, flowers, and leaves. Frankincense, myrrh, sage leaves, copal resin, spices, tree bark, and floral essences have all been used as offerings to the gods, and in more modern times custom mixtures have been developed to enhance the efficacy of spells and rituals. But so often there are fillers such as bamboo and saw-dust that can dilute or even ruin the fragrance of the essential oils of the plants, and in some severe cases they can cause acrid smells or allergic reactions. Return to the "roots" of incense and create your own magical blend for the pleasure of the gods and yourself.

This great-smelling recipe is not based on any particular spell or need; it just demonstrates how to blend assorted fragrance strengths and how to use a mortar and pestle to grind various ingredient textures. Burn it on a charcoal block, throw it into the fire, simmer it in some water, or mix it into a clay project.

YOU'LL NEED:

    Small mixing bowl
    1 tablespoon cinnamon
    1/4 cup dried orange peel
    Mortar and pestle
    3 marble-size pieces of frankincense, myrrh, or copal (or
        equivalent smaller pieces)
    5 star anise pods

Into a small mixing bowl, pour the cinnamon. Pour about 1/3 of the orange peel into your mortar (depending on its size) and grind it into a fine powder; then pour it into the bowl. Continue grinding until all the peel is powdered, and add to the bowl. Now grind the frankincense resin to a powder and add to the bowl. Finish with the star anise pods, then mix all ingredients thoroughly. Store in an airtight glass or ceramic jar.

BOTTLE CAP AND BEAD SISTRUM

It's surprisingly hard to find just the right Y-shaped stick, and I spent about a half hour finding the willow branch I used for my example project. Try using a branch with particularly colorful bark, such as redbud, willow, or dogwood.

This is an easy project if you leave the bottle caps in their natural state. Experiment to see which brands make the best sound (I especially like the way Bass caps sound), and try altering them by removing the labels and even hammering them to get more of a bell shape.

YOU'LL NEED:

    1 Y-shaped stick, about 10 to 12 inches long
    About 20 assorted bottle caps
    Hammer
    Medium-size nail (larger than the 16-gauge wire)

1 yard 16-gauge brass wire
About 12 assorted large beads
Wire cutters
Needle-nose pliers

You want a sturdy stick that is comfortable to grip in your hand and has a perfect Y for you to string the caps on. Cut it to the right dimensions while green, then allow the bark to dry on the branch at least a week before making your sistrum or the bark could come off. It's also ideal to gather your branch in the fall rather than the spring to ensure that the bark will stay in place over the years (in spring the rising sap causes the bark to be loose).

Using the hammer and nail, punch a hole in the center of each bottle cap large enough to let the caps rattle freely. Securely wrap one end of the wire to one side of the branch about 4 inches up from the fork. String on a couple of beads, then string on four or six bottle caps (whatever fits best) so that the wavy edges face each other in pairs. Finish with a few more beads and pull the wire taut, wrapping it securely around the other side of the branch, then cut off the excess wire.

Repeat the process about 2 inches from the top of the branch, this time stringing beads, then four bottle caps in facing pairs, then another couple of beads, four more bottle caps, and finish as before with beads. Stretch the wire very taut (without breaking the branch!) and wrap securely to finish. Cut off any excess wire and make sure to push any sharp wire ends tightly against the wood with the pliers. (For illustration of finished project, see color-photo insert.)

SEASONAL WREATH

Aside from greeting visitors at the door, the circular wreath is symbolic of the Wheel of the Year and the never-ending cycle of life. For a totally natural effect, make your wreath from dried leaves, mosses, flowers, seed pods, feathers, grasses, and other everlastings. Alternatively, for brighter colors and better weather durability, make yours from silk leaves and flowers. Instructions and materials are given for the Spring wreath pictured in the color-photo insert, but you can certainly make a wreath for Samhain with little skulls and black flowers, for Lammas with miniature loaves of bread and clusters of wheat, or for any holiday you like. In the materials list, "dewdrop" refers to the type of silk flower that has permanent acrylic "dewdrops" clinging to the petals—perfect to suggest a fresh Spring shower!

YOU'LL NEED:

> One 12-inch wreath base (straw or grapevine)
> Wire cutters
> 1 large cluster or 9 individual silk ivy picks
> Glue gun (low temperature is better)
> Glue sticks
> 3 silk pussy willow branches
> 1 medium cluster silk forsythia branches
> 1 3- or 4-inch bird nest
> 1 package faux mushrooms
> 2 small silk "dewdrop" iris picks
> 3 small silk "dewdrop" tulip picks
> 1 mixed color silk pansy pick
> 2 small silk "dewdrop" narcissus picks
> 1 small mushroom bird
> 1 package extra-small speckled eggs
> Several small fluffy feathers to line nest
> Large paper clip or heavy wire for hanging (if your base needs
> a hanger)

If using a straw wreath base, remove plastic and shake off any loose straw. Use the wire cutters to snip apart the ivy cluster or clip the individual ivy stems to the length you want. Arrange ivy around wreath, putting more near the bottom, wrapping around the edges as ivy might climb naturally, and overlapping the branches to help hide the cut ends. Glue securely with glue gun. (If the hot glue is melting your stems, apply glue, wait 15 seconds, then attach stems.)

Next add three pussy willow stems on the left side, tucking the cut ends into the ivy. Over this, layer some forsythia branches, then add one or two forsythia branches to the right side. At center bottom, add the nest at about a 30-degree angle, making sure it doesn't stick out past the back of the wreath base. Use the wires to secure it to the wreath; then glue (if no wires were included with your nest, use paper clips or heavy twist-ties). Add two mushrooms, one under and to the left of the nest, the other on the right side of the wreath.

Tuck one iris and one tulip into the ivy on the left side, and two tulips and one iris on the right side of the wreath. Tuck the pansy cluster under the nest. Add the two narcissus picks to the right side to balance the yellow of the forsythia.

Arrange the bird and three eggs in the nest, holding the wreath upright to see how they will look when hanging. Glue the eggs in place and then the bird. Arrange and glue a few curved feathers inside the nest as a lining. Feel free to add bits of string or more feathers to make it look even cozier. Remember to remove all glue "cobwebs" when finished.

If necessary, add a hanger to the wreath base. I used a paper clip by bending it into a V shape, then making hooked ends, then pushing the hooks up into the straw securely. (For illustration of finished project, see color-photo insert.)

HEAD GARLANDS

When doing a large public ritual, garlands are a great way to designate members of the cast or key personas in a mystery play. This Harvest Mother garland was created for a Fall Equinox ritual, so I made sure to include plenty of wheat, autumn oak leaves, and even some grapes down the back. The Dark Mother had a garland as well, featuring green-black eucalyptus leaves, black feathers, frost-tipped pine sprigs, a small crow, and even a fuzzy Halloween tarantula. Feel free to use the basic technique described here to make your own magical creations.

YOU'LL NEED:

    1 coat hanger or 20 inches of 16-gauge wire
    Wire cutters and pliers
    1 package natural raffia
    Glue gun and glue sticks
    1 bunch dried wheat
    1 bunch dyed and glycerin-preserved oak leaves
    1 bunch small dried chili pepper branches
    1 package or bunch love-in-a-mist pods
    1 bunch ivory baby's breath with added glitter
    1 bunch artificial grapes with leaves
    1 package milkweed pods
    1 floral wired dragonfly

Begin by cutting the coat hanger or wire to the measurement of the wearer's head plus about 3 inches. Twist the wire into a circlet just larger than the head circumference, making sure the cut ends of the wire face away from the wearer.

Gather a bundle of raffia about 1 inch in diameter, make one end roughly even, and tie the even end onto the wire where the back of the garland will be. Divide the raffia into three strands and braid it around the wire so that it becomes one unit, then tie off the braid next to the first raffia knot. You can secure these knots with glue if you like. Let the long strands of extra raffia hang down; they will drape over the wearer's back beautifully, like hair, and act as a backdrop for the grapes.

Witch Crafts

Beginning in the front, attach two heads of wheat (on stems) so that the long beards overlap and cross each other. Tuck small oak leaves under and around the heads, but not so that they're obscured. Continue adding oak leaves, overlapping them, until you reach the center back. Now add wheat in the same way, overlapping the stems to hide the ends and tucking them among the oak leaves. Make sure the beards of the wheat all face toward the center front. Now add some chili peppers and love-in-a-mist pods here and there, pointing these toward the front as well, and finally add the baby's breath in little sprigs. You'll be surprised how much subtle beauty this little bit of glitter will add to the overall look of the garland.

At center back, tie on the bunch of grapes with a few strands of raffia, letting them hang down over the extra raffia. On top of the leaves but not completely obscuring them, glue milkweed pods, more small oak leaves, love-in-a-mist, peppers, and so on, wiring in the dragonfly for the finishing touch on top.

GOURD RATTLE

In both Africa and the Americas, gourds have been recognized as the perfect rattles that they are: The hard shells make a loud but warm sound. Some Native American tribes fill their traditional rattles with the stones from around the mouth of an anthill, seen as gifts from the earth and the underworld. If you are running short of large anthills, however, you can use beads, small stones, or even buckshot to fill your rattle. The feathers on top fly your prayers up to the Great Spirit.

YOU'LL NEED:

    1 dry gourd, about the size of an orange (not the warty
      decorative kind)
    Small hand miter or craft saw
    Small hand keyhole saw
    Small hand drill (1/6-inch or 1/8-inch bit)
    1 straight, sturdy stick for the handle
    A handful of sharp stones
    1/2-inch-wide strip of thin suede, at least 12 inches long
    Glue gun and glue sticks
    A small handful of stones, beads, etc.
    A few dyed marabou fluff feathers
    Assorted acrylic paints and brushes (optional)

Depending on the shape of your gourd, either saw off (using the craft saw) or drill a hole in the bottom end (stem end). Using the keyhole saw, enlarge the hole to the diameter of your stick about 5 inches from the smaller end. Use the end of your stick to remove the seeds and dried pulp from inside the gourd. Place a small handful of sharp stones inside and shake very vigorously to remove even more loose material; then pour out the stones and dust.

Drill a hole in the top end (blossom end) of the gourd and enlarge it to the diameter of the smaller end of your stick. Insert the stick so that the top end sticks out about 1 inch to check fit, wrapping the suede around the stick as needed for a secure fit. Attach the leather with hot glue. Pour in the beads (or stones, buckshot, etc.) and insert the stick. Secure with hot glue.

Wrap the bottom joint between the stick and the gourd with more suede to create a smooth transition, stretching and gluing the leather into place. Repeat with the top joint, this time adding two or three feathers inside the leather wrapping as you glue it. Paint the gourd with acrylic paints if desired. (For illustration of finished project, see color-photo insert.)

RESOURCES

American Gourd Society
317 Maple Ct.
Kokomo IN 46902-3633
www.americangourdsociety.org

There are many local chapters of this national organization, which can be found on its very informative Web site. Friendly members will help you find, learn about, and enjoy gourd crafts.

Dallas Bonsai Garden
P.O. Box 551087
Dallas, TX 75355
(800) 982-1223
www.dallasbonsai.com

This store has an amazing selection of bonsai supplies, including hard-to-find books, clippers, wire, plant seeds, moss spores, and a galaxy of pots.

Flower Depot Store
P.O. Box 654
Tonganoxie, KS 66086
(877) 780-2099
www.flowerdepotstore.com

This company offers top-quality wreath-making supplies, such as twig bases, dried floral materials, and other accessories.

Witch Crafts

Keuka Flower Farm
3597 Skyline Dr.
Penn Yan, NY 14527
(315) 536-2736
www.driedflowersdirect.com

Three antique barns house over two miles of dried flower lines on this family farm. They sell retail and wholesale, and their Web site features a searchable database of dried flowers, grains, herbs, pods, greens, and more.

New England Bonsai Garden
914 S. Main St.
Bellingham, MA 02019
(508) 883-2842
www.nebonsai.com

This is another good supplier of bonsai supplies, especially unusual pots, stands, and figurines. You can buy finished trees and seedlings from them as well. They ship anywhere in the continental United States.

The Complete Book of Gourd Craft by Ginger Summit and Jim
  Widess, Sterling Publications, 1998, ISBN 1887374558

There are many inspirational ideas and designs in this extremely comprehensive book. It is a must if you're interested in exploring what can be done with these hard-shelled squashes.

Country Living Handmade Wreaths by Arlene Hamilton Stewart,
  Hearst Books, 1998, ISBN 0688161359

Great for beginners who have never crafted a wreath before and for experts looking for inspiration, this book provides clear instruction as well as ideas for using unconventional materials in all kinds of wreaths.

Quick and Easy Topiary and Green Sculpture by Jenny Hendy,
  Storey Books, 1996, ISBN 0882669206

You'll find lots of instruction and information on how to design, create, and grow living topiaries in this book.

7

FAUNA

Carved antlers that depict hunting scenes date back to the Ice Age, and the use of animal products to make items both necessary and lovely recedes back into the mists of time before that. Most scientists believe that the mammoth was hunted to extinction by Neanderthals, but this was not merely wanton destruction—every portion of the animal was used. Food, clothing, tools, and even house frames were gathered from the massive bodies of the mammoth, just as the Native Americans of the plains used every part of the buffalo and many other animals. People who lived in more lush regions, such as the tropics and along the coastlines, also used animal parts in purely decorative and ceremonial ways, especially bird feathers, turtle and sea shells, porcupine quills, and anything else brightly colored or that could be dyed easily.

SKIN AND BONES

Leather is simply the processed skin of an animal. It can be made into suede (tanned, soft, the top layer of skin removed to reveal fuzzy nap), tooling leather (smooth and somewhat stiff vegetable-tanned skin without hair), lining or latigo (thin and supple chrome-tanned skin without hair), rawhide (untanned hard skin without hair), and fur (soft, tanned with the hair on). Smaller animals usually yield thinner, softer skins that are used for linings, clothing, suede, furs, and so on. Cowhide is the leather of choice for making tooled designs, saddles, bags, and other tough articles.

Besides the skin, other durable animal parts, such as bone, horn, or antler, and even hoofs or toes, are used worldwide for many varied tools and crafts. Antlers and horns evoke a strong imagery of the Horned God, and deer or goat toes make excellent rattles. Turtle shells are also favored by some Indian tribes to make ceremonial rattles, a reflection of the belief that America is really the back of a great turtle, or Turtle Island. Porcupine quills are used by both Native Americans and Africans for decoration, to pierce the skin for ritual tattooing, and for other traditional uses.

Another animal with quills is the bird, but these quills form the centers of feathers rather than a spiny defense. Feathers have been a popular and colorful decoration in every culture in the world, are used to top Native American rattles to fly prayers to the Great Spirit, and have been used to write down our ancestors' most important historical documents. Birds have flown into world mythologies as well—from the quetzal bird comes Quetzalcoatl, the great feathered serpent of South America, and the luxurious green quetzal feathers were reserved only for royalty. Feathers can be the stiff flight feathers of the wing or the soft down of the breast. They can curl and flash like an ostrich or peacock tail, or they can shine and glimmer like a mallard's wing or a hummingbird's head.

TOOLS AND SUPPLIES

If you'll be working with leather, you'll need some basic tools. If you're just starting out, you might want to get a good basic kit that should have most items you'll need for most leatherworking projects, especially tooled leather. Such a kit might include a swivel knife for cutting tooling designs, an edge burnisher, a pair of leather scissors, punches for making stitching holes, stamps for making designs, a rawhide mallet, and perhaps a book on leatherworking basics and a few patterns.

For stitching leather, you'll want to get special leather needles, the right threads, and perhaps a sewing palm in addition to an awl and/or a small punch set. The two basic kinds of needles are the eyed glover or harness needle and the two-prong needle, which holds flat lacing in prongs rather than through an eye. What you'll be stitching with might include artificial sinew, heavy waxed thread, or flat decorative lacing in various colors.

One question I'm often asked is, "Where do you get your deer antlers?" If you don't know any hunters willing to give you some, look in the yellow pages and give your local taxidermist a call. Taxidermists are a great resource for many kinds of animal parts, and they'll often give you things like large fur scraps for free. Also ask about tanned skins that were never picked up by flaky customers; you'll find some real bargains (but make sure you know what the market price is first). Most antler racks of any size end up as trophies, but eventually people tire of them as a wall decoration and sell them at flea markets and yard sales. I got all my antlers secondhand, never paying more than five dollars for a pair. You might also check Internet auction sites for bargains.

Many colors of dyed feathers are available at craft stores and Indian supply shops, but a little-known source of truly unusual and colorful feathers is a fly-fishing store. These shops carry supplies for making hand-tied flies and have everything from small packets of peacock tail strands to entire pheasant skins ready for plucking and choosing the exact feathers you want.

THE PROJECTS

EASY KEY FOB

This simple key fob is easily decorated in a million different ways if you don't like my pattern. The words are from a Paiute Ghost Dance song and seem particularly appropriate for keys, especially car, boat, or airplane keys.

You'll need:

    1 key fob kit (round or close to round in shape)
    Carbon paper
    1 fine-tip black permanent marker
    3 wide-tip colored markers (I used red, yellow and
       purple)
    Clear leather sealer

Easy Key Fob: pattern

If your kit is unassembled, decorate and seal the leather before assembly. Reduce or enlarge the pattern (see illustration) to fit your key fob; then transfer the lettering only to the leather with carbon or graphite paper. Trace the lettering with the fine-tip black marker. Follow the lettering with the yellow marker, rather like using a highlighter pen, to draw the spiral shape. Underline the lettering and yellow spiral with a purple spiral, starting farther left than the beginning of the lettering and ending in the middle with a large dot. Outline the fob with the red pen, and color the raw edges red as well. Seal and assemble if necessary.

SIMPLE SUEDE POUCH

This pouch is quick and easy to make, especially if you stitch it up on a sewing machine that can handle heavy materials like canvas. Decorate your pouch with whatever fits your mood or purpose. The number of uses for such pouches is infinite, as are the variations of how you can make and decorate them.

YOU'LL NEED:

> Suede leather scrap at least 3 by 6 inches
> 1/2 yard suede thong (matching color or cut from same scrap)
> Leather or heavy kitchen scissors
> Button/carpet thread (matching leather color if possible)
> Shells, metal charms, crystals, beads, other decorations (optional)
> Artificial sinew and/or white glue (optional)

Examine the piece of suede for flaws and thin spots and note the "nap" if any (one-way direction of the leather grain). Making sure the halves will turn out the same, cut out two equally sized pieces (plus a 1/4-by-12-inch thong strip, if you have enough extra leather). If one side of the leather looks better than the other, consider this the "right side" and place the pouch pieces right sides together. Stitch around the curved edges 1/4 inch in from the edge, leaving the top open.

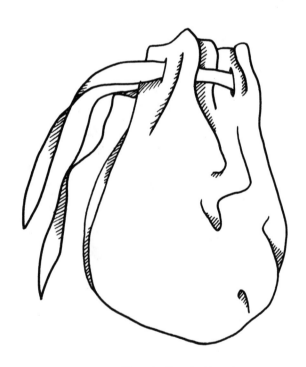

Turn the pouch so that the stitching is on the inside, and carefully snip four slits just below the top of each side for the drawstring thong. (Don't cut too close to the top edge.) Stitch decorations with sinew on one side of the pouch, adding glue if needed to secure stones, gems, mirrors, etc. Thread the thong through the slits and tie the ends together in a knot.

Simple Suede Pouch

HOOF AND HORN RATTLE

Imagine a warm summer night bardic. You begin to sing, rattle in hand, and catch a glimpse of someone just outside the firelight. . . . Could it have been a man with antlers? The essence of the Horned One permeates this musical instrument based on a California Indian traditional rattle.

YOU'LL NEED:

Coping saw
1 deer antler, base intact
100-grit sandpaper
8-1/3 yards thin suede thong or a 1-by-20-inch strip of thin suede
30 cleaned and dried deer or goat toes
Small drill or Swiss army knife with awl blade

Saw a 6-to-8-inch piece from the base of the antler for the handle. Sand the edges of the cut end of the handle to eliminate any sharp burrs if necessary. Cut the thong into 18-to-20-inch lengths (or cut the suede strip into five equal strips) and cut both ends of each thong into tapering points. Tie each thong onto the base end of the antler securely with a square knot.

If the toes are not already drilled, drill a small (1/16- to 1/8-inch) hole in each toe to admit the leather thong. I found that the awl blade of my Swiss army knife was the perfect tool for this, but a very sharp hand drill will work as well. Use extreme caution for this step since the blade can slip on the hard surface of the toe! Do not use a craft knife (like Xacto) since the blade is too thin to spin around in the hole and will likely snap off.

Thread three toes on each thong, making a knot after each toe to prevent them from sliding back off. You'll get a louder sound if the toes are separated slightly from each other on the thong. To play the rattle, hold the handle parallel to the ground and either snap your wrist sharply on each beat or let the toes drop as a cluster into your other hand. (For illustration of finished project, see color-photo insert.)

GOD AND GODDESS RATTLE

This project is based on the Hoof and Horn Rattle. Cowrie shells are a symbol of the Goddess (specifically her vulva, and thus her creative powers) in many cultures, especially Africa. The shells make a softer, almost oceanic sound, so instead of trying to be heard over the drums at a bardic, use this rattle for shamanic healing work or rituals where the room is otherwise quiet.

God and Goddess Rattle

YOU'LL NEED:

Coping saw

1 deer antler, base intact

100-grit sandpaper

8-1/3 yards thin suede thong or a 1-by-20-inch
    strip of thin suede

40 small cowrie shells, predrilled if possible

Small drill or Swiss army knife with awl blade
    (optional)

Follow the directions for the Hoof and Horn Rattle (above) for preparing the antler handle and leather thongs. Drill or carefully enlarge predrilled holes in the shells if necessary to allow the leather thong to pass through. Slide four shells onto each thong and tie a knot after each to prevent them from sliding off.

SHAMAN SAGE STAFF

Staffs can be used for many purposes, from simply walking aids to ceremonial centerpieces. Our eclectic women's coven uses a ceremonial carved staff as both a symbol of office for the Chancellor and as a tool to cast the sacred circle on occasion. This staff reflects the male energies and wisdom of the Sage, the male counterpart of the Crone.

YOU'LL NEED:

Drill with a bit slightly smaller than the diameter
    of the threaded rod

1 large staff, cut to length

1 deer antler

Epoxy

3-inch double-threaded rod

Assorted wing feathers

Sewing needle and thread

Embroidery floss, perle cotton, other interesting thin fibers

Assorted beads

Tacky craft glue or glue gun and glue sticks

8-by-10-inch piece thin suede or smaller scraps

2-by-10-inch strip of white rabbit fur

Drill a hole into the end of the staff and another hole into the antler, each hole deep enough to accept half the threaded rod. Squirt a bit of epoxy into each hole, and screw the rod into place securely. To make the bundle of feathers, bunch them together as desired and run a needle and thread through the shafts to help secure them. Drill a small hole in the top of the staff and thread with floss, or wrap some floss around the antler tines and then thread some interesting beads on the floss. Attach the feather bundle at the end of the bead strand and wrap the feathers with embroidery floss or other fibers.

Use the craft glue to attach and wrap the suede around the grip area of the staff, adding contrasting scraps as desired. Wrap the leather grip with strands of floss or other strong fibers in whatever patterns you like. Glue the strip of rabbit fur to the top of the grip area. (For illustration of finished project, see color-photo insert.)

CRONE STAFF

The image of the Crone that lives in my head is a wizened old woman, her long gray hair and dark robes blowing in the moonlit breeze, her gnarled hands clutching a sturdy staff for support or for power. A raven sits on her shoulder, and her cloak is trimmed with fur; the shells around her neck rattle like colorful bones . . .

YOU'LL NEED:

> 1 staff, cut to length
> 8-by-10-inch piece of suede or suede scraps
> Tacky craft glue or glue gun and glue sticks
> Leather needle
> Embroidery floss, perle cotton, other interesting thin fibers
> Assorted beads and shells
> 6-inch piece black fringe
> Feathered blackbird or small raven
> 2-by-12-inch piece of black rabbit fur

Around the grip area of the staff, glue your suede scraps in place. If you're using one large piece as a grip, use the leather needle to lace the area together where the edges meet. Add shell fringe to the bottom edge of the suede grip by stitching through the leather, stringing on some beads, then a shell (we used large clam shells found while beachcombing). Then go back through the shells and tie off the thread under the edge of the leather.

About 2 inches from the top of the staff, glue on the black fringe and trim off the excess. Thread assorted beads onto the fringe and tie off. The feathered bird should have a wire or some way to attach it. Wrap and glue the wire to the top of the staff or otherwise glue the bird down securely. Wrap the rabbit fur around the top of the staff once or twice, gluing into place.

Shaman's Headdress

SHAMAN'S HEADDRESS

One year at the Reclaiming Spiral Dance in San Francisco, the most amazing woman was one of the main priestesses. Her name was Sequoia, and she was dressed all in furs with the most magnificent headdress of furs and owl wings. As the lights dimmed and the ritual progressed, it became more and more difficult to tell the woman and the animal apart. I have only seen two other examples of women like this, and though they are as elusive as the wild creatures that are a part of them, their spirits are also as strong and wild.

YOU'LL NEED:

18-inch-round piece of 2- to 3-ounce suede or pigskin
Leather punch
1 yard round suede or braided string lacing
Pair of antlers on a flat piece of skull
4-by-8-inch piece of heavy felt
Glue gun and glue sticks
Artificial sinew or other heavy waxed thread
Leather or sharp tapestry needle with a large eye
2 or 3 whole rabbit skins
1 whole deer skin, preferably with tail
Assorted beads, feathers, shells, etc. (optional)

Lay the suede circle on the wearer's head and mark where the lacing should go for a secure fit (over the eyebrows and back under the base of the skull). Punch an even number of holes around the edge of the circle where marked. (Don't cut a slit instead of punching a hole because the slits can tear out under the wear of the tight lacing.) Weave the lacing in and out of the holes, ending with the lacing coming out the holes on the rough side of the suede (if there is a rough and smooth side to the leather). Try the cap on to check fit, lacing tightly, crossing the lace to the front of the cap, and tying it tightly to fit. If necessary, punch another set of holes to adjust the size or make it fit multiple wearers. Place the antlers on the top of the cap, and mark where you want them to eventually sit.

Fold the felt in half, gluing the halves together. Glue the felt to the cap where the antlers will be placed. Clean the antler skull section if necessary with an old toothbrush or other bristle brush. Measure out about 1 yard of the sinew, and thread the needle so that the two ends of the sinew both go through the eye. Wrap the sinew around the base of one antler and lock it tightly by sewing through the loop at the end of the thread. Position the antler and plunge the sinew down through the felt and suede layers. Go back up at the other antler and wrap the thread around it very tightly. Lay the thread across the skull to the opposite side and go down again. Come up on the other front corner and lay the thread across the skull to make an *X*. Keep crisscrossing across the skull until it is securely stitched down to the suede and felt base, then tie off the end. Use some hot glue to additionally secure the base to the skull.

You may wish to trim off the white edges of the rabbit fur or any ragged pieces to make a nice edge. To make an invisible cut for any kind of fur or hair-on skin, use narrow sharp scissors and slide the tip against the leather as you cut so that you are cutting underneath the hair, not through it.

Try the cap and antlers on again and position a rabbit skin on either side. Feel free to make cutouts so that the furs fit around the antlers, if necessary, and add a bit to the front to help hide the lace. When you're happy with the arrangement, use plenty of hot glue to secure the furs in place. When attaching the rabbit or other furs, avoid attaching anything at or below the level of the lacing, since you will need to crisscross that lace for a tight fit underneath the furs. Hide the lacing all you like, but don't interfere with being able to use it.

Now cut the deer skin roughly in half horizontally, giving you a tail half and a front-leg half. Trim any bare spots along the white edge (belly) or cut off the white edge completely. Fit the tail half to the back of the felt and suede cap, folding the top cut edge so that it curves around the sides and overlaps the rabbit skins. Cut out V shapes (darts) in the top edge so that you can fit it to the cap better, and use copious amounts of hot glue to hold it in place.

Try the headdress on again to fit the final piece in place. The top half should be arranged so that the front-leg sections fall to the front of the antlers and approximately where the previous layer of deer skin and the rabbit skin overlap. The remainder of the top half should cascade over the back of the antlers and overlap the first deerskin piece. Cut slits into the sides of the piece to allow the antlers to come through with fur, overlapping the base of the antlers. Use this slit as a hinge to arrange the fur, overlapping the rabbit fur on the sides and covering the side edges with the front legs. The fur should always overlap in a natural manner, front to back. Use lots of hot glue to hold everything in place.

Stitch down any parts that need extra strengthening with the sinew, making sure not to trap any fur in the stitches so that they're invisible. Add beads, fringe, feathers, shells, etc. for additional decoration, if desired. Due to the weight of the headdress, you might wish to use extra padding on top of your head if you plan to wear it for more than about fifteen minutes, so that the hard skull and antlers don't become uncomfortable.

QUILTED-LEATHER BOOK OF SHADOWS COVER

You can use any color of leather you like for this project that slips over a regular binder. If you like, you can also use the quilting technique on the inside flaps for added strength and beauty. You'll need a strong sewing machine to get through the layers of leather and quilt batting. I used the pentacle quilting design from the "Quilting" chapter for this project, but you can use any simple line drawing you like.

YOU'LL NEED:

    14-by-24-inch piece of colored latigo or garment leather

    14-by-36-inch piece of black lining leather

    Lacing punch

    White glue

    14-by-24-inch piece of extra-loft quilt batting (or two layers
       of regular batting)

    White or ivory machine quilting thread

    Black latigo or decorative lacing

    Lacing needle

    3-ring binder

Cut the garment leather to size, about 3/8 inch larger all the way around than the cover of your binder opened up flat. Cut the lining leather into one large piece the same dimensions as the garment leather and two pieces the same height and 4 inches wide (three total pieces). Lay the two large pieces on top of each other and punch lacing holes along all four edges. Punch lacing holes in three edges of the smaller pieces, using the first set of holes as a guide for the smaller pieces.

Use a tiny amount of white glue and attach the quilt batting to the wrong side of the colored garment leather; then attach the lining in the same manner, lining up the punched holes and trimming the edges of the batting as needed. When the glue has dried thoroughly, transfer the quilting design onto the lighter colored piece of leather and machine-stitch along the lines. Line up all the lacing holes and lace together the edges of the cover plus the two interior flaps. Open up the binder and fit the cover over it. (For illustration of finished project, see color-photo insert.)

TOOLED-LEATHER GREEN MAN GUITAR STRAP

This spectacular Green Man design is based on a thirteenth-century woodcarving in Poitiers Cathedral. The project is extremely time-consuming, but the final result is quite memorable. Special attention must be paid to the shading diagram for a realistic three-dimensional effect. This project is not recommended for leather-carving novices, but if you have an artistic eye for detail, have done some leatherwork before, and practice your cutting and stamping techniques first, you should do fine.

YOU'LL NEED:

   5-ounce thickness tooling leather, 6-by-37 inches, plus practice
      scraps
   Leather shears or sharp craft knife
   Leather punches: 1-3/16 inches (or 1 inch) oblong, 5/16 inch
      round
   Heavy board for punching on
   2 clean household sponges
   Small dish for water
   Blunt or small ball-tip stylus
   Swivel carving knife
   Spoon-shaped stylus
   Small crosshatch-pattern leather stamps:
      Square beveler
      Round beveler
      Triangular beveled figure carver
      Pear shader
   Rawhide or polyhead mallet
   Waterbase leather antiquing dye
   Cotton swabs
   Acrylic craft paint in kelly green
   Wool dye daubers
   #4 round soft paintbrush
   Waterbase clear sealer finish

Cut out the two pieces. Then punch the 2 round and eleven oblong holes as shown on the pattern (see illustration). If using a 1-inch oblong punch, you will need to punch the holes twice to achieve the correct width of 1-3/16 inches.

Place one of the sponges in the water dish and add enough water to make the sponge wet but not dripping. Enlarge the tooling pattern to the correct size, wet the leather with the sponge so that it is dark and supple, and lay the pattern on top. Line up the edges carefully to match the leather: Try using your fingernail to crease the edges of the pattern to

Tooled-Leather Green Man Guitar Strap: pattern
(Enlarge 170 percent)

Note: Portion at right and large portion at bottom
combine to form one pattern piece. Attach
them at the first slot.

Witch Crafts

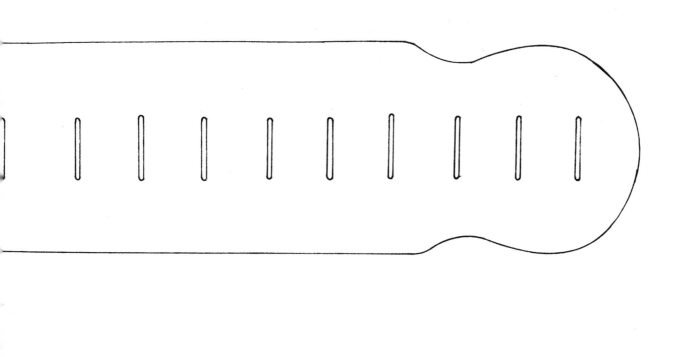

conform to the edge of the leather. Trace the pattern with the ballpoint or blunt stylus, pressing very firmly so that you leave an indented line wherever there is a line on the paper pattern. Keep the leather wet (but not sopping) when doing any stylus, cutting, or stamping work. Remove the pattern and compare it with the leather to be sure that all lines have been transferred.

To use the swivel knife, place your index finger in the top cradle and "steer" the knife blade around curves with your thumb, middle finger, and ring finger knuckle. Your pinky can be used to steady your hand for intricate cuts. Press firmly, but not so hard that you cut deeper than the top tooling layer of leather. Always hold the knife upright at a 90-degree angle to the leather surface, angling the blade at about 20 degrees toward you for cutting. Keeping the leather damp, follow and cut all the indented stylus lines.

Pressing very firmly with the blunt stylus, carefully follow all the leaf vein cuts, parting the leather and creating an indentation. If the leather pulls and distorts too much, it's not wet enough. Use the spoon stylus to curve the inside corners of the eyes, giving a rounded, three-dimensional effect to the eyeballs.

Carefully following the shading diagram, start with the square beveler stamp and begin to outline the leaves and parts of the face, overlapping the edges of the stamp to give a smooth, shaded line. Use the round beveler where necessary inside tight curves. When executing a tight V-shaped corner, use the square beveler closely inside the corner, then position the triangular beveler where the lines meet and strike firmly with the mallet for a nice sharp corner. Use the pear shader to stamp areas farther away from the beveled lines. A technique that helps overlap the stamp marks and give an evenly shaded or beveled area is to sort of "float" the stamp and move it along while gently tapping with the mallet. Keep the leather wet; if it seems like you're having to hit the stamps harder and harder to get any shading, your leather is drying out.

When all the tooling is finished, use the antiquing dye as directed on the package to give a nice shaded, three-dimensional effect. You might wish to use straight dye on a cotton swab in some areas that you want to be really dark, leaving it on rather than wiping it off. Mix the

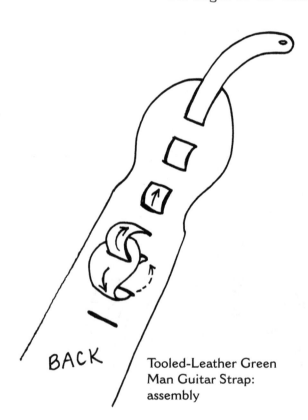

BACK

Tooled-Leather Green Man Guitar Strap: assembly

Witch Crafts

green paint with a little water to thin it to the consistency of milk. Begin painting at the tips of the leaves, blending with more and more water as you near the middle of the leaves to fade the color out gradually. When all painting has been completed, use the clear sealer according to the package directions and allow to dry completely. Assemble the parts as shown, adjusting to fit by using the various slotted holes. (For illustration of finished project, see color-photo insert.)

RESOURCES

Eidnes Furs Inc.
HC 04 Box 14
St. Maries, ID 83861
(208) 245-4753
www.eidnesfurs.com

Eidnes has the most amazing selection of furs and animal parts I've ever seen. Whether you want moose antlers, bear bones, lynx claws, or a good old-fashioned buffalo robe, this place has it all.

The Leather Shop
1482 Madison Ave.
Memphis, TN 38104
(901) 728-5551 (local)
(877) 728-5551 (outside Memphis)
www.shopforleather.com

This store has an interesting selection, including lots of remnant packs, snake skins, videos, unusual stamps, and even real zebra skin rugs! If you can't find it at Tandy, try these guys.

Matoska Trading Company
PO Box 2004
Yorba Linda, CA 92885
(714) 921-1098 or (800) 926-6286
www.matoska.com

Matoska (which means "white bear" in Lakota) has a very wide assortment of Native American craft goods, including furs, feathers, shells, beads, bells, and imitation claws and teeth. They also offer music, books, videos, shirts, finished items, and too much more to list here.

Old Style Trading Company
P.O. Box 129
South Bend, TX 76481
(940) 362-4379
www.oldstyle.net

Among other powwow and mountain man supplies, Old Style carries deer toes, drilled cowrie shells, unusual furs, sweetgrass braids, and more.

Pacific Western Traders
P.O. Box 95
Folsom, CA 95763-0095
(916) 985-3851
http://www.pacwesttraders.com/beads.html

A staple of the California Indian community, Pacific Western Traders has deer toes, drilled cowrie shells, beads, bells, herbs, and traditional Indian-made arts.

Rainbow Feather Dyeing Company
1036 South Main St.
Las Vegas, NV 89101
(702) 598-0988
www.rainbowfeatherco.com

If you're looking for a rainbow of natural and dyed feathers in bulk quantities, look no further.

Springfield Leather Company
P.O. Box 3301
Springfield, MO 65808
(800) 668-8518
www.springfieldleather.com

Not the best or most exotic selection, but Springfield is actually willing to sell cut leather by the square foot rather than by the entire side. Its Web site makes pretty amusing reading, and its staff is very nice and helpful.

Tandy Leather Company
5882 E. Berry St.
Fort Worth, TX 76119
(888) 890-1611
www.tandyleather.com

The original Queen Mother of leather suppliers, Tandy recently closed all its retail stores in favor of Internet business only. Its main forte is tooled leather supplies, but it also has a great selection of books, rabbit furs, leathers, laces, dyes, hardware, and more.

Leather Tooling and Carving by Chris Harold Groneman, Dover
Publications, 1974, ISBN 0486230619

If you need detailed information on how to get started tooling and
carving leather, you need this book. It includes 39 projects and 148 illustrations for the novice or intermediate leather crafter.

The Leatherworking Handbook by Valerie Michael, Cassell
Academic, 1995, ISBN 0304345113

Here is an excellent guide to working with heavy leathers, especially
if you're interested in how to stitch or mold them into the shape you like.
Photos and illustrations accompany clear instructions for various projects,
including masks, belts, wallets, and purses.

Traditional Indian Bead and Leather Crafts by Monte Smith
and Michelle VanSickle, Eagle's View Publishing, 1987,
ISBN 0943604141

Monte Smith is widely acknowledged as an expert in making Native
American crafts, and this book is a step-by-step guide for the beginning
leather crafter who wants to know how to make traditional projects in
suede. Each project stands alone so that you don't have to read the entire
text to make one pouch, and the numerous illustrations and photos will
make it easier for you to create any of these projects.

8

WOODWORKING

Along with clay, stone, and bone, wood is one of the oldest materials worked by human hands. Called "tree bones" or "tree flesh" by some, wood for the artisan and woodworker is available in many kinds. Unless you can absolutely verify their origins, however, it's probably best to stay away from tropical woods since many are old growth and/or cut illegally from the rapidly diminishing tropical forests of the world. Domestic woods that can be vouched for or even wood that you have gathered yourself is best. Several of the projects in this chapter use plywood, so shop carefully and ask questions before you buy.

Working with wood can be very satisfying to the senses. The colors and patterns formed by the grain are pleasing to the eye, aromatic woods are like incense when used, and certainly your sense of touch appreciates a smoothly sanded surface or a glossy finish. Depending on the wood you choose to work with, the material itself can have spiritual significance, whether oak, cedar, ash, holly, or birch is sacred to you.

Always pay attention to what the wood is trying to tell you. As Roy Underhill, host of the television series *The Woodwright's Shop*, once told me, "Modern woodworkers try to machine the stuff like it's a block of aluminum or cheese. It's not—it's a living thing." Don't ignore the qualities of your wood; work with them. Work with the grain, avoid knots when possible (unless you're using them as a decorative accent and they won't affect the integrity of the piece), and use the right wood and tools for the job.

These projects are designed to be made with minimal tools and experience—this is not *The New Yankee Workshop* and I'm not Norm Abrams (although I was a project designer for *Popular Woodworking* for a while).

Naturally, it'll be easier if you do happen to have a wood shop, but all you need to make anything in this chapter are a circular saw, a jigsaw, and a few hand tools. Even the circular saw is optional, since you can use a crosscut saw and a rip saw together in place of it, along with a hand jigsaw, but the projects will take a whole lot longer. Always measure twice and cut once; be extremely aware of safety issues such as using safety glasses and knowing where your fingers are at all times; and have fun.

THE PROJECTS

HOLIDAY LAWN CUTOUTS

When your neighbors put up their nativity scenes, you can adorn your yard with this winter stag and Crone (easily mistaken for Mrs. Claus in conservative neighborhoods). And, of course, no one will bat an eye at your Spring tableau scene come Ostara.

Holiday Lawn Cutouts: Winter Stag and Crone pattern (Each square is 1 ft. × 1 ft.)

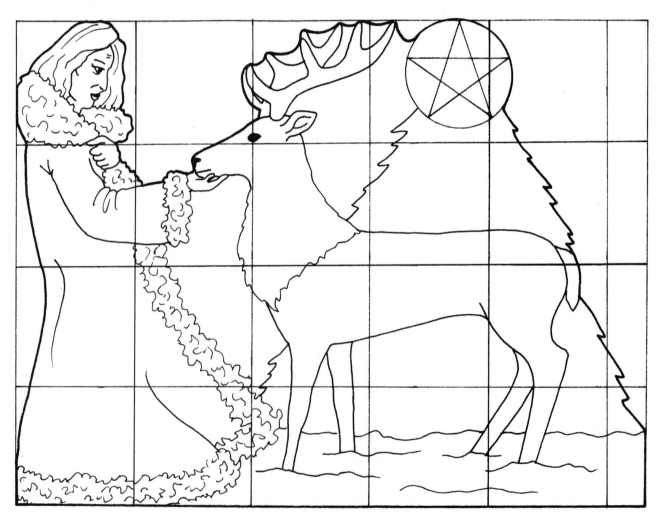

Holiday Lawn Cutouts: Spring Tableau pattern (Each square is 1 ft. × 1 ft.)

YOU'LL NEED:

    1 sheet of exterior 3/8-inch or 1/2-inch plywood

    Double-stick tape

    Jigsaw

    100-grit sandpaper

    Wood filler putty

    White primer / stain-killer paint

    Assorted acrylic or enamel paints

    Paintbrushes

    Turpentine (if needed)

    Exterior varnish, like marine spar varnish

    4 mounting brackets or 4 large L-brackets, 1/4-inch screws, and rod-type tent stakes

Enlarge pattern (see illustrations) to the desired size. Tape it to the plywood and cut along the outline of the pattern. Sand the edges smooth, fill in any holes with wood putty, and allow to dry completely. Cover with at least one coat of primer. Trace the painting pattern onto the silhouette shape and fill in major color areas. The last painting step should be the black outlines and details. Cover with exterior varnish and attach mounting brackets to the back side. Store flat indoors when not in use.

CARVED STAFF

I found a really interesting stout redwood branch while out hiking one day in the Santa Cruz Mountains, and it worked out well for carving. I have used this staff ceremonially and it feels nice in the hand. Decorate your staff any way you like.

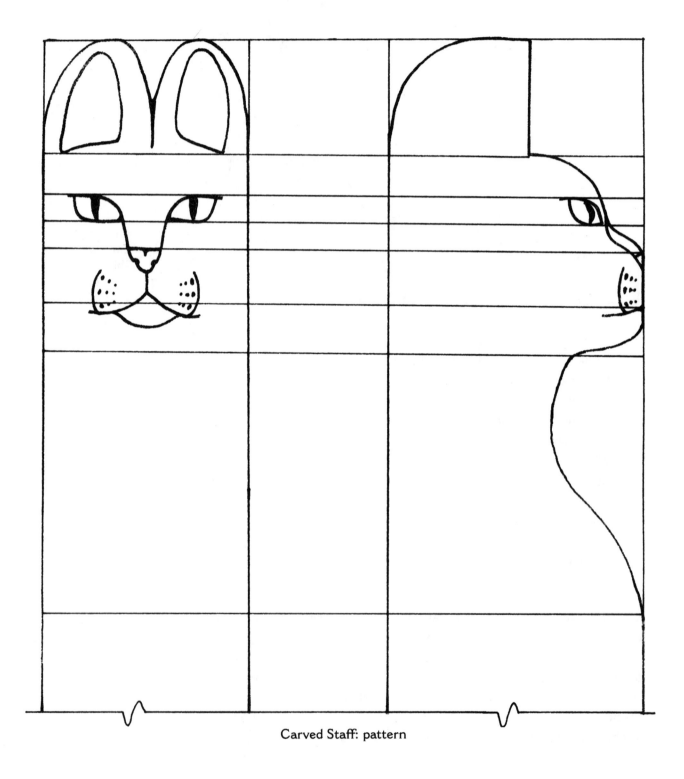

Carved Staff: pattern

Witch Crafts

YOU'LL NEED:

A stout wooden staff of lightweight yet strong wood

4 drawings of what you want to carve—front, back, and side views

Carbon or graphite paper

Various carving tools, such as a V-gouge, a 1/4-inch chisel,
    and assorted U-gouges

Sandpaper in assorted grits

Acrylic craft paints, beads, etc. (optional)

You know the old joke about how to carve a cat (or anything else)? The answer, of course, is to "remove everything that doesn't look like a cat." Well, that's actually sort of the case in carving, but you do have guidelines. Using the carbon paper, transfer the pattern (see illustration) to the appropriate sides of the staff, carefully aligning the top and bottom as well as any major graphic elements within the design. Using the flat chisel, begin to outline the design so that you are cutting down through the grain. With the U-gouge, carefully and slowly remove the wood outside these chiseled lines so that you have a crisp outline.

As you carve your design, turn the staff often to be sure everything is lining up properly and you are acheiving the dimensionality you want. Always carve away from lines, not toward them, because it's deceptively easy to slip and cut right into a major design element, and you can't uncut a piece of wood. Also, cut away from yourself and your hands when possible, exercising extreme caution and a gentle touch when you do need to cut toward yourself. Keep referring to your original drawing to be sure things are looking the way they should.

When you have the basic shape you want, use the sandpaper to do your final shaping and to smooth down the edges. Of course, you can also use chisel and gouge marks to your advantage if you're carving fur, wings, etc. Use paint if you like, as well as beads, gems, and so on for that final touch. If you will be using varnish on your staff, make sure it's compatible with your paint and that it's completely dry before you add your beads. You can use oil-based varnish over oil or acrylic (water-based) paints, but you can't use water-based varnish over oil-based paints. (For illustration of finished project, see color-photo insert.)

ROUND COLLAPSIBLE PORTABLE ALTAR

I can't tell you the number of times my groups have used these altars, both at our regular meeting places and when hosting larger rituals elsewhere. They are easy to transport, easy to set up and take down, and easy to store flat.

YOU'LL NEED:

> 1 30-inch-round or 30-by-30-inch piece of 3/4-inch plywood
> Pencil and string
> Jigsaw or circular saw
> 100-grit sandpaper
> 1 sheet 3/4-inch plywood
> White primer paint, paint of your color choice, foam brushes
>   (optional)

If making the circle, find the center of the square piece of plywood by marking a line from corner to corner in both directions, then scribe a circle by pinning a string and pencil in the center. Cut out with a jigsaw and sand the edges so that they're even and smooth.

To make the legs, cut two 24-by-24-inch squares (or the height of your choice) from the plywood sheet. Find the centers of the squares and make a 3/4-inch notch halfway up each piece to the center. Sand all edges gently and fit the legs together, forming an X. Simply set the circle on the X, and you've got an instant altar table.

SIMPLE LIDDED BOX

What could be more useful than a simple box? This project uses relatively small pieces of wood, so it might be a good excuse to get some of the more expensive or harder-to-find woods, such as holly or spalted maple, and make several as gifts.

YOU'LL NEED:

> 8-by-24-inch piece of 3/4-inch thick wood (your choice)
> Table saw (preferably with dado head, but not necessary)
> 7-1/2-by-5-inch piece of 1/4-inch plywood
> Wood glue
> 1-1/4-inch nails
> Hammer

Cut two pieces measuring 8 inches by 5-1/2 inches for the long sides and two pieces measuring 5-1/2 inches by 5-1/2 inches for the short sides. Cut a 1/4-inch rabbet on the bottom edge of all sides to accept the bottom plywood piece. Make a 3/4-by-3/8-inch dado on the ends of the long side pieces to make the short sides flush with the corners when fitted in place. Cut a piece for the top measuring 6-1/4 inches by 8 inches. Make a 3/4-by-3/8-inch groove around all four sides of the top so that it will fit in the opening of the finished box. Fit the short sides of the box into the dados on the long pieces, then glue and nail into place. Slip the plywood bottom of the box into the rabbet groove, and glue and nail into place. Finish as desired.

LOW FESTIVAL STOOL

If you don't like sitting on the ground at festivals and rituals (my back can't take it anymore), then this little stool is just the ticket. If you are very heavy, use two 3/4-inch dowels, drill out the dowel cap holes to 3/4 inch, and add two extra legs for support. The circular shape of the seat lends itself to many decorating ideas, such as the Pennsylvania Dutch Hex in the "Painting" chapter.

YOU'LL NEED:

    12-by-24-inch piece of 3/4-inch or 1-inch thick birch plywood
    Jigsaw or band saw
    Wood glue
    1-inch wood screws
    Electric drill or drill press with a tilting stage
    1/2-inch drill bit
    1/2-inch dowel
    4 dowel caps with 1/2-inch holes

Cut the plywood in half and mark on one side a 12-inch circle, plus the positions of the four leg dowels. Spread glue on one of the squares; lay the two pieces on top of each other, and, using the markings as a guide, screw the two pieces together where the screws will not interfere with the leg holes or outline of the circle. When the glue has cured completely, cut out the circle, and sand edges smooth and even. Drill four evenly spaced 1/2-inch holes at a 70-degree angle (splaying the legs outward from the center). Cut the dowel into four 8- or 9-inch sections (your preference) and test-fit into the plywood circle. Glue the dowels into place in the holes, and glue the dowel caps on the ends of the dowels. When the glue has dried completely, finish as desired.

RESOURCES

Casey's Wood Products, Inc.
P.O. Box 365
Woolwich, ME 04579
(800) 452-2739
www.caseyswood.com

Casey's has a large selection of unfinished wood components like turned dowel caps, spindles, knobs, toy parts, etc.

J. W. Etc.
2205 First St., Suite 103
Simi Valley, CA 93065
(805) 526-5066
www.jwetc.com

This company makes a variety of nontoxic varnishes, wood filler, primers, strippers, and other environmentally friendly products for the woodcrafter.

Meisel Hardware Specialties
P.O. Box 70
Mound, MN 55364
(800) 441-9870
www.meiselwoodhobby.com

This company is the only one I know of that carries lawn-ornament mounting brackets.

Popular Woodworking
F&W Publications Inc.
1507 Dana Ave.
Cincinnati, OH 45207
(515) 280-1721
www.popularwoodworking.com

This great magazine for woodworkers of all levels includes tips, projects, plans, tool basics, reviews, and more.

Tage Frid Teaches Woodworking by Tage Frid, Taunton Press, 1994, ISBN 1561580686

Whether you have never picked up a hammer or have been working wood all your life, you need this essential guide that takes you step-by-step through all the necessary techniques and tools, while offering sage advice and tips.

The Woodwright's Shop: A Practical Guide to Traditional Woodcraft by Roy Underhill, University of North Carolina Press, 1981, ISBN 0807840823

Unlike most woodworking books, this one emphasizes simplicity, working with the personality of the wood, and treating the material with respect using pre-industrial tools and techniques.

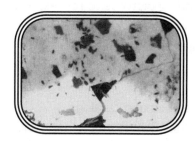

9

PAPER

As far as archaeologists have been able to determine, the ancient Egyptians invented paper around 3500 B.C.E. by pounding layered strips of Nile reeds together into a flat, thin sheet. This reed, called papyrus, is where we get the word *paper* from.

In Egyptian religion and culture, the papyrus plant was a sacred symbol of life, especially the life that came from the vitally important Nile, without which Egyptian culture could not have existed. Paper enabled Egyptians to write down songs, spells, royal decrees, and instructions to the dead for how to pass safely through the underworld. Both the substance and the use of papyrus were part of the magic, just like the book you hold now that is made from tree flesh and facilitates your sacred path.

In the Middle Ages, paper was mostly made from reclaimed rags, but today's paper is almost entirely made from wood pulp. Much of this pulp is now being recycled, and virtually all the projects in this chapter use recycled or natural materials as well.

Even today, paper is regarded in a spiritual way by some. For example, origami paper is only folded, never cut, to honor the trees that gave their lives to make it.

THE PROJECTS

INSPIRATIONAL COLLAGE

Whether you just want to make a colorful reminder of your path, honor several deities at once, or work magic through pictures and visualization, this project is both easy and fun. An informal circle I was once part of made a ritual out of making these by concentrating on what we wanted in the coming year and finding pictures to represent the fruition of our goals. The example pictured in the color-photo insert, however, is simply a fun collage of various images and deities I love.

YOU'LL NEED:

A selection of magazines and catalogs
Small, sharp scissors, such as embroidery scissors
Posterboard
White glue

Begin by selecting the pictures you'd like to use, plus some extra general images of flowers, water, trees, etc. for the background. The Sacred Source catalog is a good place to find specific deity images for this project. Keep half an eye out for how the images might be used in the finished project; you might find a photo of a diver that works perfectly with a bowl of chocolate pudding, for example.

Carefully cut out the pictures, moving and pivoting the paper rather than the scissors to cut detailed outlines. When they're all cut out, begin to arrange them on your posterboard until you have the layout you want. In my example, I cut a slit in the cauldron and inserted Ganesh as if he were coming out of it. Fill in any gaps with your background pictures of flowers and so on. When you're happy with it, glue down the back layer, then carefully attach each picture in successive layers, using only minimal glue so you don't get excess blobs marring your finished collage. (For illustration of finished project, see color-photo insert.)

DECOUPAGE TREASURE BOX

Just like the collage, this project uses images clipped from various sources and is easy to make. Let a dragon guard your treasure, or make one in honor of your favorite deity. My example, pictured in the color-photo insert, places Goddess imagery over herbs on the sides, and God forms over flowers on the lid, plus the Wheel of Fate in the middle.

YOU'LL NEED:

Papier-mâché craft box
A selection of magazines and catalogs
Small, sharp scissors, such as embroidery scissors
Decoupage medium, such as Mod Podge
Clear sealer
Acrylic paints (optional)

This project can use layers of pictures to cover the box completely, have a painted background for the images, or rely on the natural brown color of the box as a background.

Begin by choosing images from the magazines and catalogs based on the shape of your box. To cut pictures to fit the edges of your box, use the box as a template by laying it on the picture, tracing the outline, and cutting to shape on the line. Lay out your cut shapes, and when you're satisfied with the arrangement, set them carefully aside and prepare your box. Paint all surfaces, or brush decoupage medium where your background images will go and apply them. Now add your next layer, brushing medium carefully on the back of all pictures as you layer them onto the box. When all images have been placed and the box is completely dry, add a final layer of medium or clear sealer and allow to dry completely. (For illustration of finished project, see color-photo insert.)

STAMPED HOLIDAY CARDS

Sure, there are cards for Halloween and Easter (but not Samhain and Ostara), and a few are starting to show up for Winter Solstice, but what about Imbolc and Beltane and Litha and all the other special Pagan days you celebrate? It's easy to make your own colorful cards to reflect the holidays you celebrate, even if they're different from the ones the card companies recognize. If you have kids, this is great fun for them to do and helps them learn about the symbols of the seasons as well. Check out art and framing stores for interesting paper choices.

YOU'LL NEED:

> Assorted seasonal and Pagan-themed stamps
> Ink pads in a variety of colors
> Premade blank cards or heavy paper, such as parchment
> or construction paper
> Colored pens and / or calligraphy pens (optional)
> Glitter, sequins, and glue (optional)
> Unused extra greeting card envelopes (optional)

When stamping, avoid getting your fingers in the stamp pad, which can result in unsightly marks that you will only notice after you have stamped your image! Use even, strong pressure to ink the stamps. Don't rock back and forth too much or you will ink the background of the image. If you accidentally ink the edges of the nonraised area you will get an unsightly line or blob. When using older, well-used stamps that are slightly dried out, old-fashioned stamps, or metal stamping plates, a slightly padded surface (such as a mouse pad) works best. Before stamping your image, turn the stamp over and check for even ink coverage, especially with larger stamps.

A very attractive effect can be achieved with colored ink or with mixed-color ink pads. For example, fall leaves look lovely when stamped with a "rainbow" stamp pad in shades of yellow, orange, and brown. Another nice effect is to tint a card stamped in black with colored pencils. Use a firmer pencil for a "watercolor smear" effect. Be sure, however, to wait until the ink of your stamped image has dried, or you will get a different kind of smeared effect, and this one isn't pretty.

You can achieve a very nice layered effect by cutting shapes from colored paper and affixing them to a card of a different color. This can also be done in layers using more than one color. You can use a straight cut, fancy-patterned scissors that makes a decorative cut, or you can simply tear the paper for a "homemade effect." Sometimes the paper itself is fancy enough to create the card. You can also use the paper as a frame for a photo if you want to make a holiday-photo greeting card.

A word about glues: You can use a glue stick, or even white glue, to affix your papers, but a slight warping will occur. The best method is to use double-sided adhesive tape that is specially made for mounting photographs and is available commercially and through many direct sales companies that specialize in albums and stamped images.

To make the cards, start with a clean flat surface and absolutely clean hands. The card stock will pick up any little oil spot or bit of dirt on either surfaces or fingers.

The greeting card with the Egyptian image is simply wrapping paper cut to size and attached to card stock. For the sun card, choose a light color paper: If it's too dark you will have trouble seeing the image and won't be able to color it. Tear a square slightly bigger than you think will be right (you can always tear it smaller, but you can't make it bigger). Adjust the size until you are satisfied. Remember that paper has a grain of sorts. Two of the sides will tear practically straight and two will not tear easily at all. You need to take this into account as you are tearing to allow for mistakes. Stamp the sun on the torn shape, and attach the shape to the blank card. Remember to be creative: Tilt the paper or tear it into a crescent, experiment with different colors of paper and ink, and so on.

It's also a nice idea to match the card inside with the envelope, so either on the back or in the lower left corner of the front you might stamp something that hints at the card inside itself. For a fall card, for example, you might stamp a single leaf on the back of the envelope where a wax seal would have been placed.

HANDMADE PAPER WITH HERBS

This paper is great for specific magical uses. Choose herbs that amplify your needs so that they will become an integral part of your working. For example, write a wish to be free and cleansed of something on the paper you made with sage leaves inside and then burn it. To boost your creativity, sprinkle some dragon's blood powder in your wet pulp and use the resulting paper for writing poetry. The possibilities are endless.

YOU'LL NEED:

> Scraps of old paper or preshredded cotton linter
> Old blender
> Large tub or bin, such as a plastic dishwashing tub
> Herbs, spices, leaves, flowers, etc.
> Papermaking screen and deckle set
> Smooth towels or cloths, such as kitchen linens
> Rolling pin (optional)
> Iron (optional)

Tear up some old papers and soak them overnight. Run the mixture though a blender that will not be used for food (some inks are toxic and will not fully wash out). The mixture should have a texture like cooked

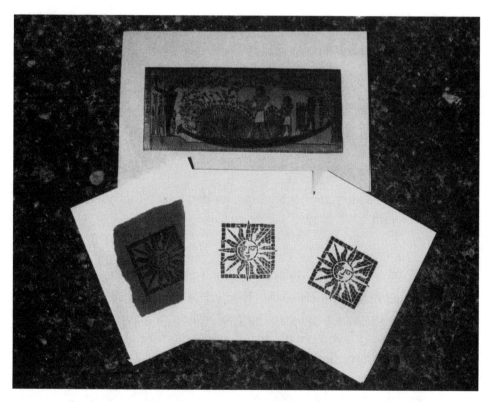

Stamped Holiday Cards (*designed and made by Karen Frank*)

oatmeal. An alternative is to buy preshredded cotton linter, which does not need to be run through the blender.

Mix water and paper pulp in the tub until the mixture resembles a paper pulp slushy. Add herbs and, if you like, bits of colored paper for decoration. Drag your mold and deckle set through the pulp until the mold is evenly covered with the pulp. Let the excess water drain off, and remove the deckle frame. Paper side down, roll the mold over a towel or piece of cotton cloth. The paper should roll off on the fabric and leave the mold clean. Place another piece of fabric over the paper sheet. Put your layers of fabric and paper sheets between a couple of towels and squeeze out the extra water—rolling over it with a rolling pin works well. Let the paper sheets dry between the fabric. They will pop off when done—or, to speed up the process, you can iron the layers on a low setting. (For illustration of finished project, see color-photo insert.)

PAPIER-MÂCHÉ MASKS

Celebrating *dias de los muertos*? Can't find an appropriate mask of your spirit animal? Going to the witches' ball? Making your own mask ensures that you'll have just what you want when you want it.

YOU'LL NEED:
> 12-inch party balloon
> Newspapers
> White flour
> Medium mixing bowl or large pie tin
> Felt-tip pen
> Masking tape
> Craft knife
> White gesso
> Acrylic paints and brushes
> Fur, glitter, tissue paper, fabric, etc. for decoration (optional)
> Cord or yarn

Blow up the balloon so it's about the same size as your head and tie off the end. Tear a section of newspaper in half horizontally, and then tear this into strips about 1 inch wide. Tear some of these strips in half. Mix about 1/4 cup of flour to about 1 cup of water, adjusting the amount of flour and water until you have a soupy paste mixture about the thickness of very heavy cream. Set the balloon horizontally in a bowl.

Dip a strip of newspaper into the flour mixture, running it between your fingers to remove the excess paste, and lay it on the balloon, smoothing it down as best you can with your fingers. Continue dipping and adding newspaper strips, crossing them over each other and overlapping the edges, until half the balloon is covered. The strips should be at least four layers thick, and no balloon color should be visible through the newspaper. Don't worry if the edges are a little ragged, but do try to keep it neat and lay horizontal strips on last for a strong edge. Let dry completely.

Check for thin spots by holding the mask up to the light, and paste on more newspaper strips if necessary. Now add a nose, ears, horns, etc., by making the basic shapes you want from newspaper. I made my skull features from little wads of crumpled newspaper. Use a felt-tip pen to mark where you want your shapes to go. With thin strips of masking tape, attach your shapes to the head. Add some dipped newspaper strips over the tape to help them stick better and become incorporated with the mask body. Keep adding strips to the nose, ears, etc. until they're the shape and size you want. Let dry completely.

Pop the balloon and trim the edges of the mask, also cutting eye, nose, and mouth holes as desired with the craft knife. Cover both sides of the mask with gesso, which will help fill in some of the newspaper lines, and allow to dry. Paint and decorate the front as desired. Poke three holes on each side of the mask, string each one with about 12 inches of cord or yarn, and braid the strands together to make ties for securing the mask.

PRICKED CANDLE LAMPSHADE

At the forefront of the Shinto pantheon is Amaterasu, the sun goddess. Let this shade, based on traditional nineteenth-century Japanese prints, inspire you while the candle burns. It doesn't matter what kind of shade your candle lamp comes with, since you'll be replacing it with the one you create. I found the one I used for the lamp pictured in the color-photo insert in the bargain section of my local craft store (the glass shade was cracked). Try looking at thrift stores for ones that are missing a shade completely. You can also find bobeche lamps designed to fit over tapers.

YOU'LL NEED:
    Inexpensive premade candle lamp
    Dark-colored construction or artist's paper
    Small self-adhesive lampshade, approximately 4-1/5 by 5 inches
    Tape
    Large towel, folded
    Large embroidery needle
    Hot glue or tacky fabric glue
    Fabric trim to match paper
    Copper or brass wire

Pricked Candle Lampshade: pattern
(Enlarge 150 percent)

Enlarge the pattern (see illustration) to the correct size. Cut a construction paper blank larger than the pattern outline. Tape the pattern on top of the construction paper and lay them together on the folded towel.

Punch holes with the embroidery needle along all pattern lines, making a series of clean holes. When finished, cut along the outside line of the pattern and carefully apply the pricked paper to the adhesive lampshade. You pretty much get one shot at this, so take your time lining it up. Make sure the seam of the shade is in the back so that Amaterasu's face is opposite the seam. Begin smoothing the paper onto the shade from the center toward the back edges. Smooth out any wrinkles carefully, using your fingernail if necessary.

Glue the edge of the paper seam down securely. Attach your fabric trim on the top and bottom to finish the edges nicely. Depending on how your candle lamp is constructed, you'll need to neatly wire the lampshade to the metal frame or cut off the bulb clip and let it sit on top. (For illustration of finished project, see color-photo insert.)

RESOURCES

Appaloosa Art Stamps

P.O. Box 85
Viola, ID 83872
(866) 882-0333
www.aasimagick.com

This store has a nice selection of Pagan and "new age" type rubber stamps, sold by the plate and wholesale as well. It also has mounting supplies, beads, and multicolored metal leaf and paper products.

Kate Cartwright

Box 824
Ketchum, ID 83340-0824
(208) 726-9609
www.katecartwright.com

Here you'll find a beautiful selection of Goddess and Pagan rubber stamps, featuring mostly traditional images from around the world.

The Paper Catalog

240 Valley Drive
Brisbane, CA 94005-1206
(888) FLAXART
www.thepapercatalog.com

A division of Flax, this family-owned San Francisco art supply house has been a regional favorite since 1938. Its paper catalog features a wide variety of truly unusual and exotic papers from around the world, from paper made with bougainvillea petals or embossed birds to hand-printed Japanese chiyogami paper and flocked florals from India (and less esoteric selections as well).

Tear It Up
1301 Wood Creek Dr.
Cedar Park, TX 78613
(888) 349-8327
www.papermaking.net

Tear It Up is a good source of papermaking supplies like molds, deckles, inclusions, pigments, casting molds, and more. Its Web site features lots of basic information and instruction, and it even sponsors a yearly papermaking convention.

Creative Collage Techniques by Nita Leland and Virginia Williams, North Light Books, 2000, ISBN 1581800983

If you liked the Inspirational Framed Collage project and want to explore more collage techniques, check out this book that starts out at the beginning level and advances through increasingly complex and intricate methods and materials.

Creative Rubber Stamping Techniques by Mary Jo McGraw, North Light Books, 1998, ISBN 0891348786

Author of several books on making rubber-stamped crafts, McGraw appears to have her techniques down and an inexhaustible supply of new ideas for enthusiasts of this popular art form.

Making Your Own Paper by Marianne Saddington, Storey Books, 1992, ISBN 088266784X

An invaluable guide for beginning paper makers, this well-illustrated little book will get you started with practical instruction on how to make paper from beginning to end.

PAINTING

Like most of the other arts in this book, painting is extraordinarily ancient, as sites around the world attest. Ancient humans from France to Australia to California all found that certain materials made colorful and long-lasting paint that could be applied to the walls of caves to create images of running animals, handprints, star charts, ceremonial drawings, and even shamanic half-human figures.

Later cultures added to the basic palette of earth pigments by using ground gemstones and dyes made from plants and insects. There's little evidence to tell us how ancient the art of plant- and animal-based paints and dyes may be because they don't have the durability of the mineral pigments like iron oxide, chalk, cinnabar, copper, lead, ochre, and various forms of carbon. But where preservation has been possible, as in tomb sites or in naturally occurring dry or protected conditions, we can discover how important painted decoration was in ancient times.

Most people don't realize that the Egyptian temples were all once brightly colored and that several thousand years of weather and sand have destroyed much of this art. Inside the tombs, however, we see bright frescoes and murals in the form of scenes from the patron's life, symbols to magically help protect the mummy, and instructions for how to pass through the underworld safely. Similarly, from Crete to South America, we see brightly painted tomb and temple scenes describing royal deeds and, less frequently, daily life and the natural world.

Ironically, until the nineteenth century, a popular dark brown pigment was made from ground-up Egyptian mummies and other unsavory or dangerous ingredients. As their effects on the human body began to be understood, pigments like white lead and cinnabar were phased out in favor of safer (and in the case of Egyptian Brown, less grisly) pigments.

Although natural pigment and oil-based paints are available for the fine artist, most modern crafters use acrylic craft paint, a water-based polymer paint that dries quickly and features very bright and lasting colors. For simplicity's sake and ease of cleanup, this chapter will use acrylic craft paints exclusively. These are the ones you can find at any craft or fabric store that come in one-ounce bottles (or larger) with a flip top.

Like pigments, the painter's brush also has natural roots, and until recently the best brushes for use with acrylic paint were almost exclusively those made of natural hair, such as camel, sable, or squirrel. Today's taklon brush, however, features the soft flexibility of the natural-hair brush with better durability and less cost (with the added bonus for vegans of not containing any animal products). Natural bristle brushes are still available if you prefer them, of course, and the stiffer synthetics are excellent for making hard-edged lines or adding texture to thick paint layers. Foam brushes are excellent for applying smooth undercoats to large areas, and by using them you avoid the streaks and dropped hair contamination often caused by cheap bristle brushes.

THE PROJECTS

PAPIER-MÂCHÉ STAR BOX

Grab a premade papier-mâché star box from any craft store and you can whip up this project in only a few minutes. Experience with calligraphy is helpful but not essential, as long as you follow the pattern carefully.

YOU'LL NEED:

> Papier-mâché star-shaped box
> Carbon or graphite paper
> Acrylic paint in white, opaque blue, opaque yellow, opaque red, and medium green
> #6 chisel blender brush
> Water-based matte spray varnish (optional)

Transfer the pattern (see illustration) to the lid of the box using carbon paper, or simply use the pattern as a reference if you feel comfortable freehanding the letters. Hold the brush at a 45-degree angle to achieve the proper calligraphy look. When you're done with the first word, turn the box counterclockwise and paint the next word, continuing until all five words are finished (the first word should be dry by this time, so you

Papier-Mâché Star Box: lettering patterns

won't smudge it when working on the last word). Finish by painting the edges of the lid in corresponding colors, as shown in the picture of the finished project. Add a matte spray varnish on all surfaces except the bottom, if desired, but the paint soaks into the paper well enough that this really isn't necessary to protect it. It's also fun to paint the inside of the box in any design or color you like. (For illustration of finished project, see color-photo insert.)

YULE TREE ORNAMENTS

Kids and adults alike love this project—it's holiday fun for everyone.

YOU'LL NEED:

> 1-1/2 cups salt
> 4 cups white flour
> 1-1/2 cups water
> Circular cookie cutter or a drinking glass
> Drinking straws
> Acrylic paints in various colors
> Assorted brushes (like a #6 round, #1 round, script liner,
>   and #4 chisel flat)
> Spray varnish
> Ribbons for hanging

Mix the salt and flour in a ceramic or glass bowl and add the water a little at a time, kneading the dough when stirring becomes too difficult. Mix and knead the dough until it can be rolled out easily, adding extra water if too dry and flour if too wet. Roll out and cut into circles; then poke hanger holes with straws. Bake on an ungreased cookie sheet at 200 degrees for at least 1 hour, checking to be sure the circles are hard but not turning brown.

When cool, paint the circles with symbols of the season that are meaningful to you—suns, pentacles, snowflakes, holly, ankhs, Kente cloth patterns, Native American or Celtic motifs, whatever you like. I chose a Pennsylvania Dutch–style rose to reflect part of my own heritage (see color-photo insert). If the paint is not fully opaque, you might need to put down a white undercoat to ensure a bright final color. When dry, spray with varnish. When the varnish is completely dry, add ribbon hangers and enjoy. (For illustration of finished project, see color-photo insert.)

PENNSYLVANIA DUTCH HEX SIGN

This project is a blending of the traditional Pennsylvania Dutch hex, found on barns and other buildings in "Amish country," and modern Pagan symbolism. My great-great-grandmother was one of the "fancy" Germans (the Amish and Mennonites being the "plain" Germans) who settled in the Midwest and became known as the Pennsylvania Dutch, bringing their unique artistic style to America. The basic comma-shaped brush strokes found in modern tole painting primarily come from Pennsylvania Dutch and German techniques.

In traditional hex signs, the symbols and colors used offer protection, a bountiful harvest, good luck, happiness, and so on. Since this project is a mixture of old and new, the colors retain their Pennsylvania Dutch meanings, two of the symbols are specifically Wiccan, and the other two are somewhat universal spiritual symbols.

Blue Pentacle: This symbol and the color blue both denote spirituality and protection.

Brown Eight-Point Star: This represents the Wheel of the Year, and brown is the color of Mother Earth.

Red Hearts: Red is the color of emotion and energy, and of course hearts are for love of many kinds—love for others, for community, of the Goddess.

Green Acorns: Green is the color of growth, and from acorns the sacred oaks grow.

Blue Circle Outline: Again, this color denotes protection and spirituality, and the circle both unifies and seals the power of the hex.

White Background: The backgrounds of hexes are almost universally white, which represents purity (and shows off the other colors, too).

This project can be painted on a round piece of plywood (available at many hardware/lumber stores) and hung outside your home, or it can be used on any circular object, such as the Low Festival Stool in the "Woodworking" chapter. If you are making a large plywood outdoor hex, use exterior enamel paints and at least two coats of an outdoor or marine varnish on all surfaces and edges to protect your artwork from the weather.

YOU'LL NEED:

Circular wooden painting surface

100- and 200-grit sandpaper, soft waste cloth, masking tape, pencil or pen

Acrylic paint in white, blue, brown, red, green, and black

Pennsylvania Dutch Hex Sign: pattern
(Enlarge 165 percent)

Witch Crafts

Brushes: 2-inch or 3-inch wide flat, 1/4-inch wide flat, #6 round,
   #3 round
Carbon or graphite paper
Water-based sealer or varnish (except if using enamels, then use
   oil-based)

Begin by sanding your wooden surface so that it's completely smooth on all sides and edges. Start with 100-grit sandpaper and finish with 200-grit for a clean finish. Use an old shirt or other soft cloth to wipe all the dust from the painting surfaces. Paint the entire wooden circle and edges white with the larger flat brush. Let dry completely.

Increase the size of your pattern (see illustration) until it fits your project, then use the carbon paper and a pencil or pen to transfer your design onto the white circle. Use tape to hold the pattern securely as you trace, and don't press too hard or you could leave indentations in the wood. Remove the pattern and carbon paper, then touch up any skips in the lines with the pencil.

Begin by painting the blue pentacle in the center with your 1/4-inch flat brush, using tape to mask off the straight lines if need be. Work slowly and carefully, then allow to dry completely. Next paint the brown eight-point star, using masking tape again if necessary for the straight lines, and allow to dry. Use the #6 round brush to paint the hearts and green part of the acorns, and allow to dry completely. Paint the black cross-hatching with the #3 round brush. Touch up any areas where the paint is not thick enough, and allow to dry completely. Apply at least two coats of your choice of sealer. (Make sure the varnish is crystal clear and won't yellow your work.) (For illustration of finished project, see color-photo insert.)

CRACKLE-FINISH DIVINATION TRAY

Whether you throw stones, bones, or runes, this convenient wooden tray will contain them beautifully. I got the basic idea for this project from the Yoruba divination trays that are beautifully carved and often rectangular in shape. I wanted to give the project a feeling of antiquity, so I used an interesting crackle finish. The layout of the actual divination pattern is my own creation, so feel free to change it to suit your needs and beliefs.

YOU'LL NEED:
   Wooden tray
   Acrylic paint in 14K gold, black, and red
   1/2-inch flat and #3 round brushes
   Crackle medium
   Waterbase clear spray varnish

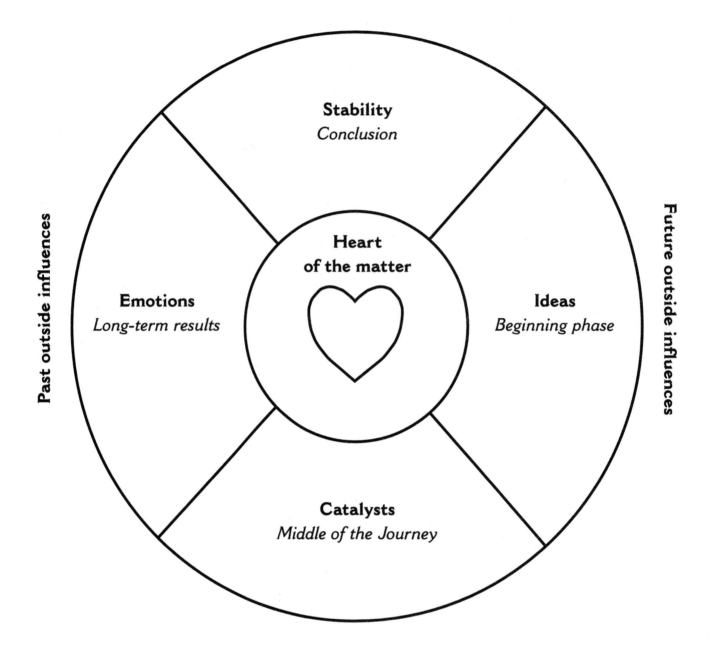

Past outside influences

Future outside influences

Stability
Conclusion

Heart
of the matter

Emotions
Long-term results

Ideas
Beginning phase

Catalysts
Middle of the Journey

Crackle-Finish Divination Tray: pattern

Witch Crafts

Paint two coats of black on the central panel of the tray, and two coats of 14K gold on both sides of the side panels. When these have dried completely, brush a medium-thick layer of crackle medium on the outsides of the side panels with the flat brush. Wait about five minutes, then load up the flat brush with black and quickly brush on a heavy layer, working back and forth without overbrushing. If you like, also take a few vertical strokes for a more varied crackle design. When this is completely dry, repeat the process on the outsides and on the panel center, using 14K gold over the black there.

When all the crackle paint has dried completely, add the red divination design (see illustration of pattern) to the tray, using the #3 round brush. Finish with a coat of waterbase satin spray varnish to protect the somewhat fragile crackle finish from chipping. (For illustration of finished project, see color-photo insert.)

OSTARA EGG

Easter is named after Ostara (or Eostre), the Anglo-Saxon or Germanic goddess of Spring. She is usually associated with a magical egg-laying hare (sound familiar? Hippity hoppity . . .) and has connections to the dawn as well as to the maiden aspect of the Goddess. Naturally, eggs have always been seen as a mystery, a seemingly dead thing from which new life arises every Spring, a powerful symbol of rebirth. This project uses a wooden goose egg, but you could certainly substitute a blown eggshell. The inscription is in Futhark, Germanic runes that pay tribute to this Lady's origins, and say "Praise to Eostre, Lady of Spring."

YOU'LL NEED:

> Wooden goose egg
> Acrylic paint in sky blue, white, opaque yellow, opaque red, forest
>   green
> Pencil
> #6 chisel blender and #1 script liner brushes
> Palette, butter tub lid, or piece of plastic
> Waterbase clear spray varnish

Paint the entire egg sky blue, using two coats if necessary to ensure even and complete coverage. Cut the rune lettering pattern (see illustration) into a narrow strip and lay it on the egg from bottom to top; then trace the outline with a pencil, creating a double line that spirals up the egg.

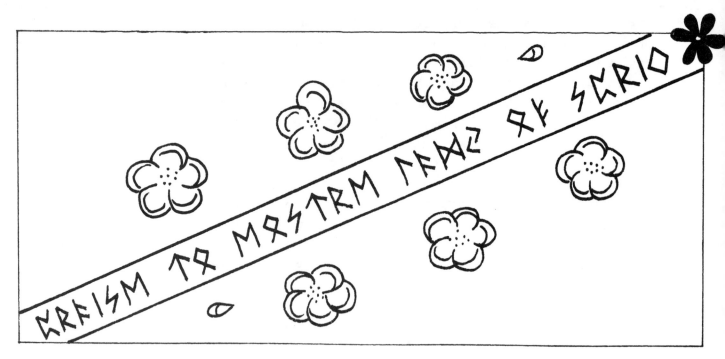

Ostara Egg: pattern

Trace the pencil lines with forest green using the script liner. When the green is dry, fill in the runes with opaque red using the script liner, and add the red flower on the very top. Add a tiny dot of white at the center of the red flower.

When all that paint is dry, prepare to paint the white and yellow flowers. On your palette (or butter tub lid, which is what I use), put down a large dot of white and, right next to it, a large dot of yellow. Double-load the chisel blender by dipping one corner into the white and the other corner into the yellow. Practice making an even stroke that is 50 percent of each color with a bit of a transparent blend in the middle of the stroke. To paint the flowers, make a pencil dot where the middle should be and place the yellow corner of the brush on the dot. Pivot the brush to make a single petal, then reposition the brush and repeat, making four or five petals and completing the flower. To make a single petal (seen at the top and bottom of the flower row), just make a tiny wedge using the same technique. Finish up each flower with seven or so tiny red dots using the script liner. Spray with varnish to protect the paint from chipping and soiling when handled.

Witch Crafts

FESTIVAL FEAST BOWL

Perfect for potlucks, this bowl will bring a smile with every serving. The large bowl I found for this project was a real bargain at my local thrift store: A little sanding to get rid of the old varnish, and the surface was ready for painting in a flash. The colors selected for the dancing people represent the nations of the world, and the poem is my own.

YOU'LL NEED:

    Large wooden bowl (pictured example is 12 inches in diameter)
    100-grit sandpaper and a soft rag
    Acrylic paint in black, white, red, yellow, brown, and green
    #2 round and 1-inch foam brushes
    Food-safe varnish (see "Resources" at end of this chapter)

Sand the inside of the bowl to eliminate any traces of old varnish, and clean it out thoroughly with the soft rag. Don't wash it out with water or this could damage the unprotected wood. With a pencil, divide the bowl into four quarters to make placing the lettering easier. Draw a line all the way around the inside of the bowl 1 inch down from the top, another line 1-1/4 inches from the top, and a third line 3 inches from the top. Either sketch freehand or transfer the pattern (see illustration) onto the bowl, adjusting to fit your bowl's size and shape, making sure to have the number of people divisible by five (fifteen, twenty, twenty-five, etc.).

Paint the text (Lord and Lady—Make us whole—Feed our bodies—Feed our souls) around the top of the bowl with green using the #2 round brush. Next paint the dancing people, alternating the colors in the same order: black, yellow, red, white, and brown. Don't worry about doing the people exactly according to the pattern—a graceful sense of movement is

Festival Feast Bowl: pattern

more important than precision. When all paint has dried thoroughly, apply a coat of varnish, then let dry. Apply a second coat, and let dry at least twenty-four hours, or follow the directions on the package before using with food. (For illustration of finished project, see color-photo insert.)

OAK-LEAF CANDLEHOLDER

The natural beauty of the wood combines with white and shades of green to highlight an oak leaf and acorn motif.

YOU'LL NEED:

Turned wooden candleholder

#1 and #3 round brushes

Acrylic paint in white, light green, medium green, dark forest green, reddish brown, grayish brown, and black

Blending gel

Paper towel

Waterbase clear spray varnish

Your candleholder might be a different shape than my example (see color-photo insert), in which case you'll need to decide for yourself where to place the white and green bands at the top and bottom. Assuming it's roughly the same shape, use the #3 round brush and paint the cup and upper part of the base medium green, the bottom of the base dark forest green, and the two bands white. You might need to touch up the edges of

Oak-Leaf Candleholder: pattern

the lines with the #1 round brush to get a clean edge. Leave the top surface of the candle cup and the middle section plain wood.

Sketch freehand or transfer the oak leaf and acorn pattern (see illustration) onto the middle section. Following the directions on the bottle of blending gel, pick up a little gel in your #1 round brush, wipe off the excess, and pick up some medium green. Fill in one leaf shape quickly and thickly; then wash out the brush, pick up some gel, wipe off the excess, and pick up some light green. Blend the light green from the tips of the leaf toward the center. Repeat with the other leaves. Using the #1 round brush paint, in leaf veins and the stem with black.

With the #1 round brush, paint the nut part of the acorn with reddish brown and the cap with grayish brown. Mix a small dot of black into the reddish brown, and draw a single line under the edge of the cap for a shadow on the nut. Seal with varnish.

TROMPE L'OEIL ALTAR TOP

"Trompe l'oeil" is French for "fool the eye", and this type of realistic painting technique has been around as long as the concept of perspective and depth. The idea is to momentarily trick the viewer into thinking that a painted area is really a half-written letter on the desk or an ivory sculpture on the shelf. The technique works best with flat objects and a photorealistic style but can be quite effective with still-life subjects painted on the back of a deep shelf or even stylized painting techniques to give more of an impressionistic feeling rather than a realistic one. This altar top is designed so that when you set your ritual items in the quarters around the sides, it appears that they are sitting on a bed of objects related to the four elements.

YOU'LL NEED:

  Acrylic paint in dark olive, white, brown, black, opaque red,
    and forest green
  2-inch foam brush
  24-inch circle of plywood
  150-grit sandpaper
  Soft rags
  Palette, butter tub lid, or piece of plastic
  Assorted brushes, such as a #6 round, #1 round,
    and #4 chisel flat
  Cup of water (for rinsing brushes)
  Paper towels (for blotting)
  Spray matte varnish

Trompe l'Oeil Altar Top: herbs pattern (North)

Paint the entire surface and edges of the plywood circle olive green. Don't worry about being super precise and covering the wood completely. When the paint is completely dry, sand the edges and the top of the wood gently to remove some of the paint, revealing a bit of the grain and giving it an old, worn appearance. Don't sand too much of the olive color away from where you'll be painting the water or it will be difficult to match the colors. Using the rags, remove all sanding dust from the plywood circle.

Transfer the patterns (see illustrations) or sketch freehand the shapes of the herbs, feathers, matches, and water. The shadowing for all the shapes is a mixture of olive and a touch of black. If it's helpful, you might want to try making your own piles of matches, feathers, etc., and painting them from life instead of following the patterns. At least try to have an

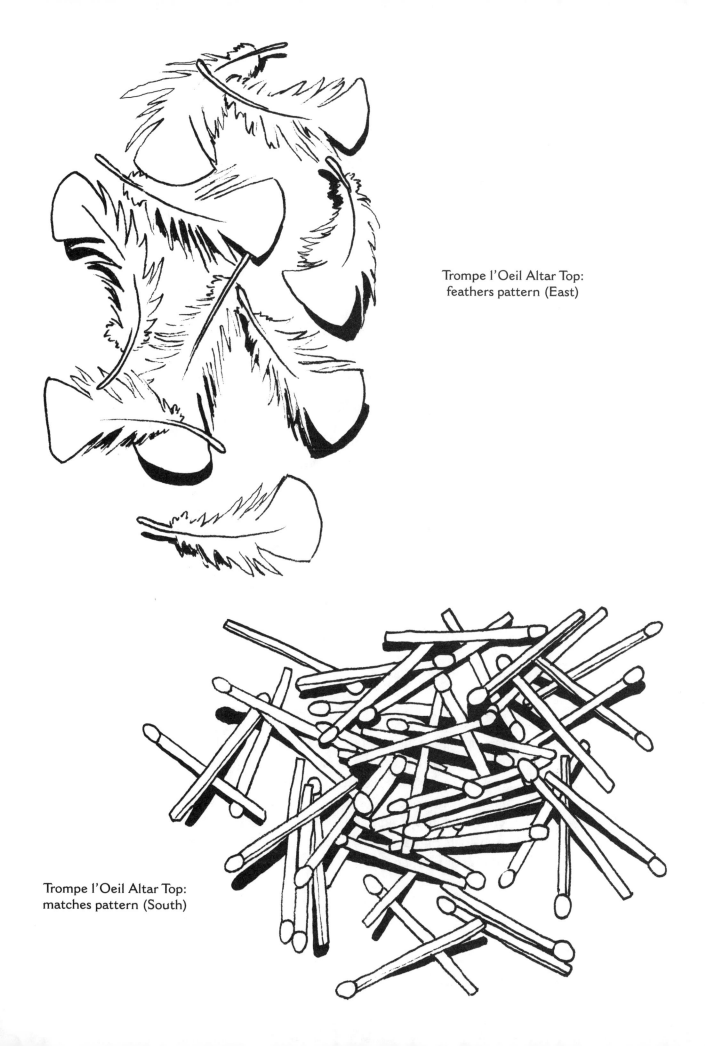

Trompe l'Oeil Altar Top:
feathers pattern (East)

Trompe l'Oeil Altar Top:
matches pattern (South)

Trompe l'Oeil Altar Top: water pattern (West)

example of each on hand to examine while following the pattern for better realism. But don't get too hung up with your painting skill or ability to make the piles look like little photographs; you're only trying to give a good impression, since anyone with binocular vision will see pretty quickly that your altar top is actually a clever painting. When you're finished, apply two coats of matte varnish over the entire surface and all edges. (For illustration of finished project, see color-photo insert.)

Witch Crafts

Eco-House Inc.
P.O. Box 220, Sta. A
Fredericton, New Brunswick
E3B 4Y9 Canada
(506) 366-3529
www.eco-house.com

Eco-House makes food-safe Dammar Varnish, nontoxic artist supplies, and other related natural chemistry products.

J. W. Etc.
2205 First St., Suite 103
Simi Valley, CA 93065
(805) 526-5066
www.jwetc.com

J. W. Etc. makes Right-Step nontoxic varnish and a variety of other safe finishes for crafters.

Plaid Enterprises
3225 Westech Dr.
Norcross, GA 30091-7600
www.plaidenterprises.com

Along with other various craft supplies, Plaid makes or distributes Folkart brand and other acrylic paints, various brands of artist's brushes, and lots of other painting supplies.

The Art of Illusion: A Tromple L'Oeil Painting Course by Janet Shearer, Northwest Regional Educational Library, 1992, ISBN 1581800975

If you need more information about how to execute a *trompe l'oeil* painting, this guide book will help you with step-by-step projects. The subject matter is generally for larger pieces, especially murals, but the "fool the eye" techniques are basically the same for large or small works.

Priscilla Hauser's Book of Decorative Painting by Priscilla Wait
      Hauser, North Light Books, 1997, ISBN 0891347224

Hauser is the founder of the National Society of Tole and Decorative Painters and her book is a treasure trove of techniques, especially for the beginner. Each brush stroke is explained, as are supplies, how to prepare surfaces, finishing, and more.

11

POTTERY

It has been said that pottery is the perfect expression of the four elements: The clay and glazes are a mixture of Earth and Water, the Air dries the clay to the right texture, and the Fire bakes the clay to make it hard. Many people don't realize that the clays we use to make such varied things as a delicate porcelain teacup or a two-hundred-pound flowerpot are used almost directly from the Earth with surprisingly little change. Each type of naturally occurring clay deposit has different properties, and you can't use delicate clays for heavy pots, nor can you use heavy brickmaker's clay for throwing dinner plates.

The term "throwing" refers to the use of the potter's wheel, which comes down to us from the Egyptian god Khnum, who created all humankind on his great potter's wheel (or from about 4000 B.C.E. in Sumeria or Mesopotamia). There are wheels run by hand, by foot, or by electricity. My personal favorite is the foot-powered kick wheel. I've found that you need a very expensive electric wheel to provide the same amount of power that a counterweight kick wheel will give you for about $100—and it's harder to control the speed. One advantage of an electric wheel is that you can let it run indefinitely if you're working on a delicate piece that would collapse if you stopped the wheel, but this extends into large art pieces that I don't find myself making. I'm a bit of a Luddite, though, and this is purely my own opinion. Many potters absolutely swear by an electric wheel, partly because of its more compact size, so you'll want to experiment and see which type works best for you.

If you prefer to use one, the kick wheel works on very simple physics. A large cement "doughnut" is anchored to a metal rod that turns a metal head, which is where you make your pots. You sit and kick the doughnut to gain speed, the wheel turns counterclockwise for a while due to the weight of the cement, and you get to work. Don't work barefoot since you'll need to use your foot to stop the wheel, sometimes suddenly if your pot is starting to collapse and you need to perform emergency surgery or if your hair gets caught in the clay (no laughing).

The type of clay used for all the projects in this chapter, with the exception of the special air-dry clay Goddess sculpture, is a gray common clay, readily available at most large craft stores and ceramics supply houses. It is one of the best clays for beginners, since it works and throws easily and is inexpensive. It fires at about 2,000 degrees and comes out of the first firing a pinkish tan.

Glazes can be mixed or purchased. It's probably better for the beginner to start off with a premixed glaze unless you have a lot of room and money to spend on many small bags of pigment, scales, buckets, and so on. You will also need a special wax that is painted on the bottom of the pot so that the glaze will not adhere and make your pot stick to the kiln shelf. A special banding wheel can be purchased for applying the wax, or you can use your regular potter's wheel to apply the wax and make stripes of colorful glaze on your pot. You can also use an old record turntable with the belt removed so that it spins freely.

As you can see, it takes a lot of investment in supplies and space to set up a pottery studio. The most expensive and space-consuming piece of equipment is the kiln. I'm not a kiln expert because I have done all my work at open studios, which is probably the best way for the beginner to experiment and learn.

There are many, many techniques for glazing your pots, including raku (my favorite!), sagar firing, salt glaze, black firing, anagama, and, of course, regular earth-pigment slip glazes. If you want to get beyond the out-of-the-jar glazes, however, there are entire books written on glazes and glaze recipes, so you should probably pick one of those up if you're serious about a future in ceramics. There is even glaze software that helps you calculate new recipes of your own based on the ingredients and colors you want.

Other tools you'll want when working on the wheel are a small bucket, several bats, calipers, an "elephant ear" sponge, a pin or knife tool, a wire loop or trimming tool, a flexible metal rib, and a cutting wire. Many of these are available packaged together in beginners' kits and don't cost much.

The bucket is for holding water, which you'll need to moisten your hands and to put clay scraps in for recycling later. Bats can be made from plaster poured into an old pie tin or from wooden circles purchased at the hardware store, and they make it easy to remove your finished pot from the wheel head without risk of damage. Calipers help you make sure that all the cups in a set are the same size or that two pieces will fit together properly. Elephant ear sponges are used to soak up extra water from inside the pot and to smooth the wet clay, and are great for helping people with long nails work with the clay, especially when first beginning a pot. The pin tool can cut off a wobbly rim or help you determine how thick your pot's base is, and the wire loop or trimming tool can carve away excess clay at the base of your pot when in the leather-dry stage (plus many other uses). The metal rib is great for making a perfect bowl and shaping a very large pot, and the cutting wire can cut a chunk of clay off your larger slab or slice a finished pot off the wheel head.

I can't describe here in great enough detail the technique of throwing on the wheel because it takes practice, finesse, practice, and more practice. Many excellent books have been written just on the basics of working with clay and throwing it, so I recommend that you check one out and perhaps even take a class at your local community college or adult education program to really learn how to throw pots properly with good technique. Having said that, I will describe a few of the basic concepts to throwing a pot with the hope that you'll get more detailed information elsewhere and then come back to make some of the more difficult projects below.

Place a bat on the wheel by flattening a ball of clay onto the wheel head and pounding the bat in place with your fist. Take a softball-size lump of kneaded clay and, using both hands, firmly slap it in the center of the bat. Alternately, you can throw directly on the head of the wheel. It won't be perfectly centered, so get the wheel turning, wet your hands slightly, and gently force the clay lump into a symmetrical and centered flattened cone shape. Now make a well in the middle of the cone with your thumbs, using the rest of your hands to hold the clay centered, and coming within about 3/8 inch of the wheel head (you can check this depth with your pin tool). Moisten your fingers as needed but do not use too much water or the clay will become too wet and collapse. Now use your fingers to open up the hole a little, forming a "volcano" shape that's about four or five inches tall. Use this basic shape as your beginning point for any form you like, whether a pinched vase or an open bowl.

After making your piece, whether it be on the wheel or freehand, you'll need to let it dry before firing it. Some studios have a room with a humidifier that slows down the drying process so that you have more time to work with a piece if you will be changing it after it's off the wheel. The stage at which this work is done is called the "leather" stage, when the piece is firm enough to be handled without damage but has not begun to get so dry that it cannot be altered. It's at this point that you can recenter your piece on the wheel and use a tool to carve a foot into the bottom of a bowl, put square sides on a bottle, or attach pieces together (for instance, a handle to a cup). Be sure to scribe your name or insignia on the bottom at the leather stage.

When the piece is allowed to dry completely, it's ready for firing—and it's also extremely fragile. Never pick up a "green" piece of pottery with one hand unless it's small and sturdy; if you do you could easily snap off a piece accidentally. Your pot will shrink by about 30 percent as the water in the clay evaporates: It's important to take that into account when making something that must fit something else, like a candleholder or a votive cup. After the first firing the piece will be a completely different color than the clay you started with and will be much stronger. Now is the time to add your stains and glazes in preparation for the second and final firing. After it cools, it's time to enjoy the beautiful results of all your hard work.

So now you've seen how the four elements work together to create pottery. But no matter how you finish or glaze or fire your work, it all starts with what you create using the body of the Earth between your hands. It's sort of like magic, isn't it?

THE PROJECTS

GODDESS SCULPTURE

Let your imagination dance as you create your own Goddess. The example I made (see color-photo insert) is a reproduction of the Venus of Willendorf, which was made from limestone in about 23,000 B.C.E. Clay was well known to Paleolithic (early Stone Age) humans, and there are fascinating examples of animals sculpted from clay or clay over natural stone outcroppings on the floors and walls of caves.

YOU'LL NEED:

> Air-dry clay, such as Das, in terra cotta or brown
> Tools, such as an ice cream stick, plastic knife, or professional modeling tools
> Decorations, such as nuts, seeds, moss, ribbons, glitter (optional)
> Photos of a historic Goddess figure (optional)
> Matte spray varnish (optional)

If you're following the design of a preexisting Goddess sculpture, try to get as many photos from different angles as you can. If you're not, you might want to close your eyes and just let the Goddess energy flow through you as you shape the clay. Work with the clay, pinching, rolling, poking, and pushing it until it becomes the shape you want. Use the tools to make folds, scribe facial features and hair, or add details like fingers or other small body parts. When you're done, allow your sculpture to dry undisturbed according to the directions on the package. You might wish to use a little spray varnish to make your sculpture easier to clean over time. (For illustration of finished project, see color-photo insert.)

SLUMP SLAB BREAD TRAY

Surprisingly simple to make, this rough-edged hand-built tray is a beautiful way to serve the Lammas bread and is a reminder of where that bread comes from, too.

YOU'LL NEED:

    1 pound clay
    Rolling pin or slab roller
    Several heads of wheat with beards
    Large towel
    Brown stain
    White gloss glaze

Make a small loaf shape from the clay and roll it out to about 1/4-inch thick, making a rough oval that's about 6 by 16 inches. Press the wheat deeply into the clay, getting a good impression of the stems and beards. Roll up the towel lengthwise and make an oval on the table, then place the slab inside so that the edges are supported and curve upward slightly, making a shallow dish. Allow to dry completely and fire. Use a dark brown stain inside the wheat shapes and overglaze with a semi-opaque white glaze, keeping all glaze off the bottom of the dish. Fire again.

Slump Slab Bread Tray (*designed and made by Jen Snedeker*)

SIMPLE EARTHEN CHALICE

This piece is actually constructed from two separate thrown pieces. I love the natural brown semimatte glaze for how it feels in my hand and how it perfectly reflects the essence of the Earth Mother in my mind.

Simple Earthen Chalice

YOU'LL NEED:

1 pound clay
2 wheel bats
Pin tool
Clay slip
Brown semigloss or matte speckled glaze

Make the stem of the chalice by making the standard cone, then narrowing the middle and opening up the lip. Set aside. Make the cup of the chalice as a round-bottomed small cup by making a small cone, putting your index finger inside, and pushing out a bulge in the middle, steadying with your other hand from the outside, then opening up the lip to a nice cup shape. Check the size to be sure it will match the stem nicely, and adjust if necessary.

When both pieces are at a soft leather stage, use the pin tool to make crosshatched marks on both pieces where they will meet. Brush some slip on both pieces and join them, moving them back and forth as you push down gently to help the clays mesh together. Allow to dry and fire. Apply the brown glaze and fire again.

CUTWORK CANDLEHOLDERS

The ways of decorating this basic bowl shape are infinite. Cut out the shapes of leaves, stars, moons, animals, or even the Goddess herself, and let the flame shine forth in the darkness.

YOU'LL NEED:

1 pound clay
Pin or knife tool
Card-stock shape templates (optional)
Any color glaze you like

Start by throwing a basic cup or globe shape from 5 to 8 inches in diameter. To do this, make the standard cone and put your index and middle fingers inside. Push outward, steadying the clay from the outside with your other hand, and open up the lip until it's large enough to admit a votive candle (plus 30 percent). When the clay is still soft, use the pin tool to cut out shapes from the sides of the pot. If you will be making many of these, you might wish to make a template out of card-stock paper and run the pin tool around the edge for completely uniform cutouts. You might also choose to deform the lip of the pot as shown by the example in the color-photo insert. The opening was made into a curvy square by pinching opposite sides together a bit. Allow to dry, fire, glaze, and fire again. (For illustration of finished project, see color-photo insert.)

LIDDED JAR

These jars are just the thing for keeping basic altar necessities—such as salt, resins, or charcoal blocks—handy and fresh in a beautiful way. The pictured example is completely smooth on top, but you can also create them with built-in handles.

YOU'LL NEED:

    1 pound clay
    1/4-by-2-by-4-inch piece
        of wood
    Pin tool
    Your choice of glazes
        and stains

Lidded Jar

Begin this pot by making your standard starting cone with a base of about 5 inches. Using your index and middle fingers, push outward to form a bulge near the base, leaving the top half of the cone the same. Now begin slowly pinching and restricting the opening of the cone while pushing down slightly to form a fat vase shape. Keep restricting the top until the opening closes completely, and either pinch the top into a knob shape or pinch it off altogether to form a smooth dome. You can use a rib or sponge to help shape the dome, but don't push down too hard or it will collapse. Use the wood to make a 1/2-inch-deep groove in the side of the pot where you want the lid to be. Poke a hole in the bottom edge of the groove with your pin tool to allow the air to equalize as the pot dries. Allow to dry to the leather stage.

Using the pin tool, slowly cut into the bottom edge of the groove, catching the lid as it separates from the rest of the jar. Clean up the edges if necessary for a clean fit. Fire. If you're careful and you're using a glaze that won't run, you can actually put the two halves together during the second firing to save kiln space (don't glaze the joint where the bottom and the lid meet). Fire again. If the halves do stick together when you're done, you can try gently tapping the edge where the halves meet while the pot is still warm to try to break the glaze that's sealing them together.

ANCIENT-MOTHER INCENSE BURNER

Based on the same technique as the lidded jar, the incense burner allows fragrant smoke to curl mysteriously from the Mother's basket. You can change the basket to a cauldron, or change the design completely to suit your fancy.

YOU'LL NEED:

> 1 pound clay
> 1/4-by-2-by-4-inch piece of wood
> Pin tool
> Your choice of glaze

Make the base of the burner in the same way as for the lidded jar (the preceding project). Make the base to measure about 6 inches in diameter and leave or cut a 1-inch hole in the top of the domed lid. Set aside and let dry to moist leather stage. Use the pin tool to make several ventilation holes in the back of the pot about 1/2 inch from the upper edge of the bottom.

When the pot is ready, sculpt your Goddess or other shape separately, making an opening in the bottom of the basket for the smoke to exit. Angle the hole if necessary so that it roughly lines up with the hole in the center of the base pot. Attach the sculpture by using the pin tool to make crosshatch marks and using a bit of slip as glue. Touch up the edges as necessary and allow to dry. Fire. Glaze the base and top portion of the pot only; don't glaze the Goddess figure or where the base and lid meet. Fire. Fill the bottom with about 1 inch of sand before using for incense. (For illustration of finished project, see color-photo insert.)

TRIPOD INCENSE BRAZIER

I actually made this to be a Water bowl, but when it was done it looked so airy that it really needed to be an incense brazier instead. The tripod is quite fragile at all stages, even when fired, so be sure you have a safe home for it in your altar supply stash. But you must agree that the effect it gives is truly stunning.

YOU'LL NEED:

  2 pounds clay
  Extruder with a "cloverleaf"-shaped die (or shape of your choice)
  Newspaper, towels, boxes, etc.
  Transparent gloss glazes of your choice

Extrude one long piece and cut into three 5-inch pieces and one 9-inch piece. Form the 9-inch piece into a seamless ring. Taper the ends of the three 5-inch pieces by smoothing them with your wet hands and pulling slightly. Crumple a little newspaper and place it in the middle of the ring, then press the three tapered pieces into the ring to attach them and make feet, letting them curve in toward the center and rest on the newspaper. Use the towels, boxes, newspaper, etc. to hold the ends of the tapered pieces so that they curve back outward gracefully as shown in the color-photo insert.

Make the bowl by opening out your cone into a bowl with a very thin edge. Use your fingers to make the edge wavy, something like a pie crust. Allow both pieces to dry completely and fire. Glaze both pieces as desired and fire separately. To use, place the bowl on the tripod, fill it with 1 inch of sand, and burn the charcoal or incense on the sand. (For illustration of finished project, see color-photo insert.)

POTLUCK CUP AND PLATE SET

How many Pagan potlucks have you been to that use paper or plastic plates and cups that get thrown away? Have you noticed how much trash that generates, not to mention the natural resources and toxic chemicals used to make the items in the first place? The environmentally friendly solution is this cup and plate set that can be used forever and also shares the sentiment "Never hunger. Never thirst." Of course, feel free to put whatever design you like on your set. Just be sure the glazes you choose are food-safe. And keep in mind that your clay will shrink about 30 percent when dry, so make these items much larger than you think you'll want.

YOU'LL NEED:

> 3 pounds clay
> Flexible metal rib
> Extruder with cup handle die (optional)
> Pin tool
> Large soft brush
> Food-safe glazes and stains in green and brown (or colors
>   of your choice)
> Clear food-safe glaze

Potluck Cup and Plate Set

Make the plate by starting with a centered lump rather than a cone, which will produce an overly thin rim. Pinch the lump in the middle of the sides so that it makes a sort of "flying saucer" shape. Pull this lump sideways slowly while also making a gently curving dish in the middle. Use the rib to help shape the inside of the plate, pushing with gentle pressure to maintain a nice concave shape. Continue pulling the sides out until the plate is as large as you like, but be careful not to make it too thin or too wide or it could collapse when you stop the wheel.

Make the cup from a simple footed cylinder with a slightly flared lip and an attached handle (or, if you prefer, omit the handle entirely). Throw the cylinder first and score it with crosshatching at the two points where you will attach the handle. Use the extruder to make the handle. If you don't have access to one, make the handle by forming a sluglike shape about the size of your thumb. Wet your hand and begin to flatten and pull the shape, running your thumb and forefinger down its length quickly. When the handle is the right size and shape, fold over the top and attach it to the cup at the scored points.

Allow both pieces to dry. Resist the temptation to pick up the mug by its handle as you load the kiln and fire both pieces. Decorate the cup with the words "Never Thirst" and the plate with the words "Never Hunger," using glaze or stain. Add any other motifs you like, and then cover with a clear glaze. Fire again.

Axner Company, Inc.

490 Kane Ct.

Oviedo, FL 32765

(407) 365-2600 or (800) 843-7057

www.axner.com

A real ceramics superstore, complete with videos, books, clays, glazes, kilns, wheels, tools, and too much more to list here. Their Web site offers some information about ingredients and their safety as well.

Big Ceramic Store

463 Miwok Ct.

Fremont, CA, 94539

www.bigceramicstore.com

Here you'll find lots of different supplies for the ceramic artist, like clay, glazes, studio equipment, and more. Some of the listings can be a bit on the technical side if you're not sure what you're looking for, but you can contact the store for help if need be.

Clay Factory Inc.

804 South Dale Mabry Highway

Tampa, FL 33609

(800) 942-0444

www.eclayfactory.com

Aside from a paper and Internet catalog with some solid basics, Clay Factory's Web site features some interesting articles. The actual store-front is an open studio, workshop, and classroom.

The Big Book of Ceramics by Joaquim Chavarria, Watson-Guptill
  Publications, 1994, ISBN 0823005089

This amazing book features virtually everything there is to know about ceramics, including clay types, hand-building techniques, kilns and how to use them, glazes and application methods, throwing on the wheel, molds and how to make them, and tons more.

Clay and Glazes for the Potter by Daniel Rhodes and Robin Hopper
  (Krause Publications, 2000)

If you're serious about your craft, especially if you want to learn how to mix your own glazes, this book is an essential classic. Originally published in 1954, the new revised edition features such updates as an expanded color section, warnings about the health hazards found in some glaze ingredients, and information about computer calculation programs.

The Potter's Wheel by Barbaformosa (Barrons Educational Series, 2000)

This is an absolutely essential book for working on the wheel, especially if you're a beginner. Packed with hundreds of full-color photos, every step of the process is shown in detail and explained with the depth of a college course.

12

GLASS

The first glass was actually made by the Earth in the form of volcanic obsidian and other minerals. It took until about 3000 B.C.E. for humans to master the creation of glass in the form of molten silica (sand), soda, and lime. The ancient Romans were really the first to turn glassmaking and glassblowing into an art form, and the first leaded stained-glass windows began to appear in the eleventh century. Today's glass is free of flaws and easy to work with, and many supplies (such as lead-free caming) are much safer to use, too. Whether you like the simplicity of etching with acid or the complex beauty of a stained-glass window, there are plenty of interesting materials on the market to keep the glass enthusiast happy.

Etching acid comes in paste form and actually eats away a thin layer of glass where applied, creating a frosted surface much like sandblasting (without the mess and expense). It's not a good material for large areas, however, because the frosted effect can turn out somewhat blotchy. Simulated stained glass uses an opaque "lead" that is applied as a very thick liquid and dries hard. Between the "lead" lines a clear liquid glass paint is used to give the look of stained glass.

Another modern glass-decorating technique is the color pen, which enables you to draw a thin line of transparent color on any glass surface. And of course, the ancient materials of stained glass and glass mosaic tiles enable you to create almost anything you can imagine in a rainbow of colors.

When working with glass, safety is an absolute must. Always wear eye protection and closed-toe shoes when cutting glass, and use solder and other chemicals with good air circulation and ventilation. Be sure of what you're doing, and practice first before attempting something you're not sure of to avoid expensive mistakes or even injury. If you've never done any glass cutting or stained-glass work, please consult a book on the subject that can lay out techniques and safety tips far better than one chapter here can do (see the "Resources" section at the end of this chapter for my book pick).

Always clean your glass thoroughly with soap and water or a streak-free cleanser before starting a project.

THE PROJECTS

TRIPLE-MOON SUNCATCHER

A premade clear-glass oval suncatcher makes this project a snap to finish in as little as one hour. The triple-moon design represents the Maiden (white), the Mother (red), and the Crone (black)

YOU'LL NEED:

> Clear-glass oval suncatcher
> Gallery Glass Simulated Liquid Leading in silver
> Gallery Glass Window Color in snow white, ruby red, and charcoal
>   black

Enlarge the pattern (see illustration) to just fit inside the frame of your suncatcher. Cut the tip off the bottle of liquid lead, making sure to start off with the smallest hole possible: You can always enlarge it if you need a larger line. Practice making an even curve with the lead, and adjust

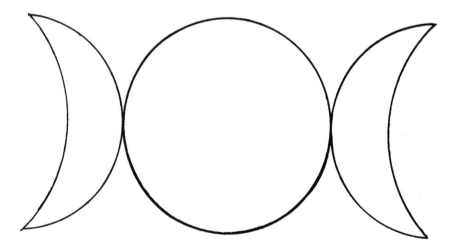

Triple-Moon Suncatcher: pattern

the size of the hole until the line is as thick as you'd like (try to match the thickness of the oval's lead frame). For a nice even line, lift the tip of the bottle about 1/2 inch off the glass surface and let the liquid draw the line for you rather than trying to touch the bottle to the glass.

Lay the glass on top of the pattern and trace the lines of the pattern with the liquid lead. Allow to dry completely, about one hour or more (it will cure more quickly on dry, hot days). Color in each area of the triple moon symbol with liquid glass stain, applying very thickly and evenly with no holes in the color. Allow to dry completely before hanging. (For illustration of finished project, see color-photo insert.)

SIMULATED STAINED-GLASS MIRROR

"Know Thyself" is an important tenet in some traditions, and I think it's a perfect sentiment to have on a mirror. The lead lines make the beveled mirror appear to be crafted of five separate pieces, and the glass gems add extra color and dimensionality to this intricate project.

YOU'LL NEED:

   8-by-10-inch beveled mirror
   Carbon paper
   Gallery Glass Simulated Liquid Leading in black
   Paper towels
   Gallery Glass Window Color in kelly green, cameo ivory, snow
      white, and ruby red
   Glass gems
   Glue gun and glue sticks
   8-by-10-inch frame

Firmly trace the pattern (see illustration) onto the mirror with carbon paper. Following the directions for using the liquid leading in the previous project, cut a very fine hole in the tip of the bottle and practice making lines. Set the mirror near the edge of a table and use the table as a guide for your hands as you trace the edge of the bevel on all four sides. Use even pressure and a steady hand. If you make a mistake, wait for it to dry, cut off the bad line with a razor blade, and try again. Also trace the four corners of the beveled edge. Allow these outer lines to dry completely.

Trace all other lead lines and allow to dry completely. You will probably need to use paper towels to blot any excess liquid lead from the tip of the bottle as you work, since this extra lead will make your lines fatter and leave blobs at the beginnings of lines. Color in the leaves, crescent, antlers, and letters *K* and *T* with glass color, applying very thickly with no

Know Thyself

Simulated Stained-Glass Mirror: pattern

holes or thin spots. Attach glass gems, as shown in the photo in the insert, in your choice of colors if desired. Place the mirror in the frame, trimming the corner leading with a razor blade if necessary. (For illustration of finished project, see color-photo insert.)

SCRATCHBOARD SUNCATCHER

Travel back to ancient Greece and gaze upon this image of Apollo with his lyre from a red figure vase. Choose a different glass color, mix several together, or use stained glass to make your own suncatcher.

YOU'LL NEED:

Rectangular suncatcher
Glue gun and glue sticks
Craft knife (like Xacto)
Masking tape
Black spray paint
Gallery Glass Window Color in turquoise (or your choice of color)
Clear fixative (optional)

Scratchboard Suncatcher: pattern

Most likely the lead border (called came) around your rectangular suncatcher will be loose at the top and bottom, so you'll need to glue it before proceeding. Just squirt some glue into the groove of the lead and press the glass into place, trimming off any excess glue when it has cooled. Mask off the lead came with the tape and spray a completely opaque coat of black on one side of the glass. When this has dried, turn the glass over and apply a thick layer of liquid glass color (turquoise or your choice of other color) to the entire surface, leaving no holes or thin spots. Allow to dry completely.

Trace the pattern (see illustration) onto the black side of the glass and use the knife to slowly and gently scratch away the black paint to reveal the color behind it. Use the tip of the knife to outline the areas you will be removing, then use the flat of the knife to remove the paint. Spray with clear fixative when finished if desired. (For illustration of finished project, see color-photo insert.)

MOSAIC STEPPING-STONE

A combination of miniature mosaic tiles, brightly colored gems, and tumbled beach glass make this image of Cernunnos come alive. The Horned God wears his torc as a symbol of his high status and is surrounded by his sacred snake symbol. There are many possibilities for variations on this project, including using real antler tips, using all tumbled glass instead of the tiles, filling the lines around his face and name with gold wire, and using different shapes of molds.

You'll need:

    1 small bag miniature mosaic glass tiles, assorted greens
    1 small bag miniature mosaic glass tiles, assorted browns
    1 small bag tumbled beach glass in browns, whites, and greens
    1 small bag glass gems
    Cement
    12-inch octagonal stepping-stone mold
    Trowel
    Craft or ice cream sticks
    Small bucket
    Water

Enlarge the pattern (see illustration) to fit the mold, and set aside. Outside, next to where you will be pouring the cement, place the pattern on the ground and weight it down so that a stray wind doesn't ruin your layout. Arrange your glass pieces on top of the pattern, choosing naturally curved pieces for the antlers and the end of the snake's tail. Use gems for the eyes and ends of the torc.

Mosaic Stepping-stone: pattern
(Enlarge 155 percent)

Mix the cement according to the directions on the package and fill the mold. Smooth the surface with your trowel, using a craft stick for a final smoothing, then shake and wiggle the mold to smooth it further. Use a craft stick to very lightly scribe the lines of the face, antlers, snake, and torc. Begin setting the glass pieces on the lines, reproducing your arrangement as on the pattern paper. When everything is arranged to your satisfaction, press the pieces into the wet cement, patting areas with the flat of your hand to settle the glass and even the cement. Give the mosaic a final check to be sure no sharp corners are sticking up, and let the cement rest for at least two days, then remove it from the mold. Scrub any excess cement dust off the glass pieces with a dish sponge and water. (For illustration of finished project, see color-photo insert.)

PAINTED VASE

Flora is the goddess of flowers, so what better way to celebrate her than with a vase? A clear glass vase works best to let the bright colors shine through the water. Try placing it on a sunny windowsill and change the water daily.

YOU'LL NEED:

Plain clear glass vase
Masking tape
Vitrea 160 glass painting pens in Sun Yellow, Amber, Pepper Red, and Bengal Pink
Acrylic craft or acrylic gloss enamel paints in various colors
#1 and #5 / 0 round brushes
Glass and tile medium (if not using enamel paints)

Enlarge the pattern (see illustration) to the correct size for your vase, and tape it to the inside. If your vase is not perfectly cylindrical, you'll need to fold or cut the edges of the paper to make it fit as closely as possible.

There are two ways to do this painting, by starting with either the black painted outlines or with the colored glass pen areas. I started by coloring in the flowers, hair, and lettering with the pens and added the outline last. Unless the pattern fits your vase exactly, you may encounter distortion problems, especially if the glass is thick or curved. Hold the pattern in place with one hand while you paint with the other to help you follow the pattern more easily. Also try shutting one eye at times to cut down on distortion. Use sweeping brush strokes and avoid overworking any strokes, as this will give an uneven or crumbly line.

To finish, bake the vase in your oven, following the directions on the Vitrea pens exactly.

Painted Vase: pattern

ETCHED VOTIVE HOLDER

These four goddesses of Fire are also from the four corners of the Earth: Oya is an African Orisha whose number is 9 (seen in her hair). Pele resides in Hawaii's volcanoes. Brigid is Ireland's triple goddess. And Greek Hestia is also known as Vesta in Rome. They are portrayed in the artistic style of their homelands (except for Pele, for whom I was unable to find a traditional image). If you don't have a square candleholder, feel free to choose just one of the images and put it on a small cylindrical holder.

HESTIA

BRIGID

◊YA

ÞELE

Etched Votive Holder:
patterns

YOU'LL NEED:

Glass votive candleholder, preferably square
White self-stick shelf paper
Xacto knife
Cotton swabs or acid brush
Armour Etch glass-etching acid paste

Transfer the patterns (see illustration) onto the self-stick paper and cut out the individual patterns to fit your candleholder. Remove the backing and carefully stick the paper onto the candleholder, smoothing out any bubbles. If you have a very stubborn bubble, prick it with a sharp needle and smooth out the air. Using the knife, cut away the shaded areas of the designs and remove the paper.

With the cotton swabs, apply a very thick layer of acid paste to the open design areas, making sure there are no holes or gaps in the paste. Do *not* touch the acid paste with your skin or breathe the fumes! Acid is a slow-acting corrosive, and you can get a bad burn before your skin ever starts to feel the pain. Allow the acid to work for about five minutes.

Carefully wash off the acid paste under running water. Feel free to use your hands now to rub it off the glass, as the water instantly neutralizes the acid. Remove the paper and dry your new work of art. (For illustration of finished project, see color-photo insert.)

STAINED-GLASS WINDOW HANGING

The faerie star, or septagram, is a symbol to both practitioners of Faerie Wicca and to those with a fae nature at large. This design features lots of straight lines and outside curves, so it's a beginner-to-intermediate pattern. If this is your first project, you might want to practice with some easier designs first to get the hang of it, or just take your time and learn

while you go if you're not afraid to give it a try. At the very least, famil-
iarize yourself with soldering techniques and materials before undertak-
ing this project.

YOU'LL NEED:

Stained glass in your choice of colors
Low-pile carpet sample square
Spray adhesive or double-sided tape
Glass cutter
Glass nipper pliers
3/8- or 1/4-inch lead H and U came
Came cutters or sharp diagonal snips
Soldering iron
Flux-core solder
Short section of metal chain
Shop or hand-held vacuum

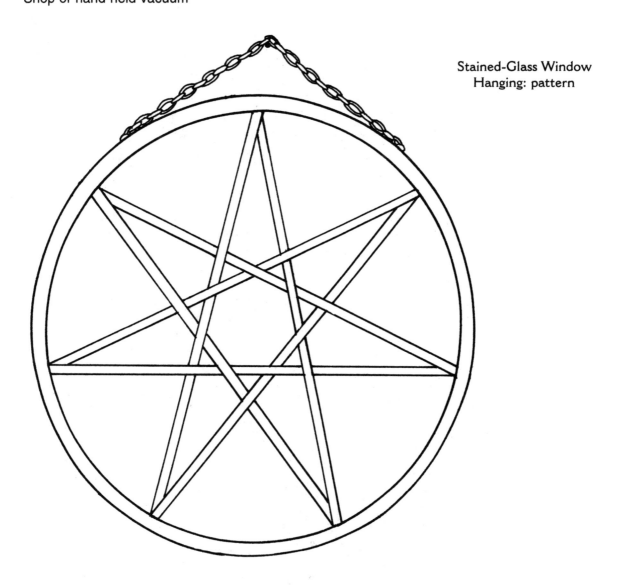

Stained-Glass Window
Hanging: pattern

First and foremost: *Always* wear safety glasses when you're cutting glass. Now, find a work area where stray pieces of glass won't cause injury, such as a garage, workshop, or outdoors. Make two copies of the pattern (see illustration) in the desired size. Cut one into pieces and tape the other to a table near your soldering area. The one you're cutting apart should accommodate the thickness of the lead.

Use a very light spritz of spray adhesive on the backs of all pattern pieces to ensure that they don't move around when cutting your glass. Place your glass on the carpet sample, which will help contain the tiny bits of stray glass while you cut it. Following the main pattern, stick one pattern piece to the appropriate color of glass and closely follow the outline with the glass cutter. Remove the pattern piece, break out the glass piece, and place it on the main pattern to check the fit. If the fit is off far enough that it crowds an adjacent piece or will cause a gap, you'll need to nip off, sand down, or even recut the piece. Continue until all glass pieces are cut.

Cut a piece of H came to fit one side of the center piece, and press the lead firmly into place. Keep fitting pieces of lead into place, overlapping the edges and checking against the original pattern, until the entire design is finished and everything fits snugly. You might need to snip the came to fit at an intersection if too many pieces of lead are causing a bulky joint. Add a piece of U came around the entire outside circumference of the circle. If the pattern was enlarged much past 9 inches or so, you might need to use nails around the outside edges to help hold the pieces firmly together while soldering.

Beginning in the center, solder the lead joints in place, making sure the iron is the proper temperature to give a nice smooth joint. Continue soldering until all joints are neatly and securely connected, then carefully flip the entire piece over and solder the other side. Solder on a length of chain for hanging your piece, then clean the glass thoroughly to get rid of the greasy solder flux residue. When you're done, and especially if you were working inside, vacuum up any stray bits of glass.

RESOURCES

Mad Mosaic
5028 S. Ash Ave., Suite 104
Tempe, AZ 85282
(480) 456-0364
www.madmosaic.com

This small company offers an amazing selection of mosaic tiles, glass gems, other supplies, and information.

Plaid Enterprises
3225 Westech Dr.
Norcross, GA 30091-7600
www.plaidenterprises.com

Along with other various craft supplies, Plaid makes the Gallery Glass line of simulated stained-glass products.

Stained Glass Warehouse
97 Underwood Rd.
Fletcher, NC 28732
(828) 654-8778
www.stainedglasswarehouse.com

Here you'll find kits, tools, supplies, books, and even free patterns! It's hard to imagine what stained-glass supplies these guys don't have. They also carry Vitrea glass painting pens.

Glass Painting in an Afternoon by Mickey Baskett, Sterling
    Publications, 2000, ISBN 0806922990

Here's a comprehensive guide to painting on pre-made glass objects such as lampshades, cups, plates, vases, and more. Many techniques and materials are covered, and crafters of all skill levels will enjoy this book.

How to Work in Stained Glass by Anita and Seymour Isenberg
    (Krause Publications, 2000)

This is the best book I've ever seen on getting started in stained glass. It's written for the beginner and contains lots of amusing anecdotes and tips, as well as information on various techniques and materials.

Mosaic Stepping Stones for Beginners by Roy Kapp, RAK
    Publishing, 1999, ISBN 0967369827

Kapp combines the arts of mosaic and stained glass in this book, which features how to make concrete stepping stones with cut stained glass pieces.

Index

ABOUT THE AUTHOR

Willow Polson is a born-and-reared Californian, and has been a self-initiated Witch since the age of thirteen. She has enjoyed writing and fiddling with all manner of arts and crafts since she was a little girl, especially embroidery and candle making. Her major at San Francisco State University was art, with emphasis in ethnic arts. She has studied anthropology as well. Other interests include various fiber arts (she makes traditional California Indian-style baskets, as taught to her by Pomo weaver Julia Parker), living history, organic gardening, vegetarian cooking, and working on her mountain homestead near Yosemite National Park.

Willow is one of the co-creators of *Veggie Life* magazine, and has been on the staff of other internationally popular magazines, including *Needlepoint Plus*, *Tole World*, and *Popular Woodworking*. Her own publishing venture, *Recreating History* magazine, featured articles on historic crafts, period foods, and how to be a better historic reenactor. She is currently a member of the National Needlearts Academy and the Society for Creative Anachronism's West Kingdom Needleworker's Guild, as well as the Pagan Educational Network, Witches Against Religious Discrimination, Pagan Unity Campaign Political Action Committee, and other Pagan rights organizations. Willow is also a member of the Pagan Educational Network, Alternative Religions Educational Network, Sacred Earth Alliance, and Pagan Unity Campaign, and is a supporter of The Witches' Voice.

The Polson family's long-term goal is to build a castle, complete with courtyard, great hall, portcullis, and secret passages. For further info, tips, news, craft ideas, recipes, and more, visit www.willowsplace.com.